HIDDEN TREASURES

BIRMINGHAM VOL II

Edited by Lynsey Hawkins

First published in Great Britain in 2002 by
YOUNG WRITERS
Remus House,
Coltsfoot Drive,
Peterborough, PE2 9JX
Telephone (01733) 890066

HB ISBN 0 75433 792 8
SB ISBN 0 75433 793 6

FOREWORD

This year, the Young Writers' Hidden Treasures competition proudly presents a showcase of the best poetic talent from over 72,000 up-and-coming writers nationwide.

Young Writers was established in 1991 and we are still successful, even in today's technologically-led world, in promoting and encouraging the reading and writing of poetry.

The thought, effort, imagination and hard work put into each poem impressed us all, and once again, the task of selecting poems was a difficult one, but nevertheless, an enjoyable experience.

We hope you are as pleased as we are with the final selection and that you and your family continue to be entertained with *Hidden Treasures Birmingham Vol II* for many years to come.

CONTENTS

Hobmoor Primary School

Holly Clayton	73
Samantha Fry	73
Lisa McCusker	74
Katie Rose	74
Maxine Quayle	75
Stacie Genders	75
Laura Hoult	76
Kate Robinson	76
Emma Wakelin	77
Laura Pollard	77
Kelly Gillam	78
Ashley Reading	78
Charlotte Busby	78
Lyndsay Smylie	79
Beth Rose	79
Melissa Smylie	79
Geila Alpion	80
Athena Sanders	80
Kerry Martin	81
Andrew Spurrier	81
Zoe Davies	82

St Dunstan's RC School, Kings Heath

Brogan France	82
Ailish Erin Prosser	82
Leah Costello	83
Connor Kelly	83
Michelle Simone Clark	84
Jessica Stait	84
Alex Carmichael	85
Stephen Martin	85
Louis Jobanputra	86
Andrew Martin	86
Rachel Wallace	86
Marcella Frances Rose Meehan	87
Charlotte Kinzett	87
Victoria Edge	88
Ryan Malanaphy	88

St John's CE Primary School, Sparkhill

Rema Blake	89
Rhianne Locke	89
Philip Davis	90
Henna Panchal	90
Matthew Evans	91
Adam Wheatley	91
Nathan Numan	92
Hiteshree Kundalia	92
Shiro Miller	93
Vishal Thanki	93
David Andrew Weake	94
Jamie Mullis	94
Zarha Ali	95
Rozie Corbett	95
Nathan Delfouneso	96
Stefan Michael Wrobel	96
Heena Jagatia	97
Chloë Lee	97
Robert Ashley	98
Lydia Smith	98
Kina Sinclair	99
Jerome Greaves	99
Naomi Bishop	100
Anika Parmar	100
Haifa Choudhury	101

Stanville Primary School

Joseph Greenfield	101
Nathan Lowe	102
Chantelle Evans	102
Abigail Barter	103
Michelle Ball	103
Mica Pencheon & Shabana	104
Sean Berwick	104
Reece Willett	105

Uffculme Special School

Adam Teeling	105
Luke Satchwell	106
Steven Taylor	106
Adam Sutcliffe	107
Leon Ming	107
David Walsh	108
David Eling	108

Wheelers Lane Junior School

Amar Kundhi	109
Lewis Williams	110
Luke Whitehouse	110
Tom Reilly	111
Stefanie Brown	112
Aimeé Schörnig-Moore	112
Kieran Child	113
Jack Reed	113
Lucy Blyth	114
Natasha Durrani	114
Chris Evans	115
Lisa Reilly	115
Raghav Jogia	116
Caitlin Anderson	116
Eloise Foley	117
Lucy Burns	117
Scarlett Sprigg	118
Daniel Howell	118
Joshua Wilson	119
Carla Hancox	120
Anjali Unarkat	120
Yousaf Kharal	120
Robert Williams	121
Nicholas Parry	122
Yasmin Moseley	122
Jennifer Barnes	123
Jade Brooks	123

The Poems

DROPLETS FROM HEAVEN

Dark clouds form in the sky,
The sound of thunder brings forward the storm,
The light changes to darkness,
The wind blows stronger

Slowly, slowly the lightning breaks the darkness,
Tap, tap the rain goes, waking the Earth,
Dancing and shimmering with the sunlight,
Droplets of water fall from the sky.

The sound of the stream,
The currents of water get stronger and stronger,
Tap, tap goes the rain,
Bringing life again,

Suddenly the rain stops,
The Earth sponges all the water,
Puddles are left behind,
Glowing like gold capturing the autumn sun,

The Earth brings life,
The birds fly high and sing,
Heaven is now the Earth,
We rejoice in the miracle of life.

Kiran Saleem (10)
Arden Primary School

TELLING

One, two, three, four
Telling Miss, Gary swore.
Five, six, seven, eight
Now I haven't got a mate.

Kashaf Ali (9)
Arden Primary School

BUGS AND CO

I like Bugs Bunny
Cos he's so funny
He likes those carrots
From Mr Scarrots.
I like them too
I even ate a few
They were so yummy
They filled my tummy
Now *Bugs* is my mate
Tomorrow we'll skate
When *Porky Pig* comes
We'll show him hard sums
He'll go *crazy*
Eating the *daisy*
Now we are friends
So
We'll be called *Bugs & Co!*

Arshad Hussain (10)
Arden Primary School

PICNIC

Cloudy, cloudy sky
On a day that
Should have been dry.
Packed a basket
Full of food.
Looked at the sky
And started to cry.

Through the clouds
A ray of light
Which made my heart
Jump in delight.
Grabbed my coat
Opened the door
Hello sunshine
Where shall we go?

Asha Shazeen (9)
Arden Primary School

THOUGHTS

I don't have a name,
Or body to feel.
I'm always invisible - not really real.
You won't know which flower smells best,
Which food is your favourite,
Or when you need rest.
I can make you laugh hard
About jokes that you heard,
Or wrinkle your brow,
When you can't spell a word.
If you help get your friend
Out of a muddle
I make you feel warm - like a toy that you cuddle.
I can make you afraid of
Bumps in the night,
So spooky and scary,
You wake with a fright.

Faisen Rahman (10)
Arden Primary School

IF I COULD DO WHAT I WANT

If I could do what I want I would punish the teacher
When she destroys our lives
By not teaching us how to count in fives
And when she shouts at my friend Jake
When he can't bake.
I would punish the children by shouting
When they don't do their schoolwork for homework.
Imagine me allowed to sit by the creek
Not just by an ugly freak.
Imagine me doing what I want!

Afreen Akhtar (10)
Arden Primary School

SUN

The sun is set
When the sun set
Evening is all around
The sun is rising
Morning is all around
I go to school
When the sun looks at me
I come home
When the sun is walking with me
I love the sun and the sun loves me.

Kanwal Raza (10)
Arden Primary School

SHOPPING SATURDAY

I look on my calendar
Saturday's here.
I put my hands on my head
And shout 'Oh dear! Oh dear!'

It's more shopping this weekend
For me and my mum.
She stuffs things in her basket
While I stand there feeling glum.

She touches ornaments and dresses
And feels a blue and yellow mat.
I just look at a pathetic painting
And she shouts 'Don't touch that!'

We go to many other shops
And buy loads and loads of things.
By the time we get out of the jeweller's shop
She's covered in bracelets and rings!

At last it's time to go home
But something happens on the way.
Mum meets a friend
And they talk to the end
Of this terrible Saturday!

So now you know how shopping
Is really terrible for me.
Until next week to shop some more
I'll be completely free!

Maryam Qureshi (10)
Arden Primary School

SPOOKY

He slithers like a tiger in the tall grass,
His tail gives a sharp flick in the sun.
His ear gives a twitch very fast,
His whiskers fan as he starts to run.

He is as black as the night sky,
He is silky and silver.
His eyes are gold dishes as he passes by,
In the cold nasty wind his fur gives a quiver.

He jumps through the window and laps up his cream,
And his little bell tinkles.
He curls up by the fire and snoozes and dreams,
When he wakes he stretches and yawns, his eyes twinkle.

He twirls and curls in ribbon and wool,
Dancing and playing on the rug.
He jumps on my lap when I sit on the stool,
He purrs like an engine when I give him a hug.

Usman Muhammad Malik (10)
Arden Primary School

PENNY POEM!

I had five little pennies
Going to the shop,
Enough for some sweets
But none for pop.

One sweet for Mum,
One sweet for Dad
And one for my brother
Who isn't so bad.

One sweet for teatime
Leaves one sweet for me,
Should I eat it right now
Or . . . hmm delicious!

Henna Sabir (9)
Arden Primary School

WELCOME TO THE HAUNTED HOUSE!

Step in through the rusty gates
Be quiet as a mouse
We're going to sneak and take
A peek inside the haunted house!

Ghosts are hooting in the hallway,
Ghastly ghouls lurk on the stairs,
Imps and sprites have pillow fights
To catch you unawares!

In the kitchen there's a wizard
Making slug and spider pies.
They're for a very special meal,
A Hallowe'en surprise!

Upstairs in the dusty bedrooms
Skeletons are getting dressed.
Vampires must brush their hair and teeth,
All the spooks must look their best!

So while the party's in full swing
Be quiet as a mouse.
Tiptoe out while you still can
Escape the haunted house!

Suhenaz Sultana (9)
Arden Primary School

MY HANDS

My hands are part of my body
And they are guided by my heart . . .
My hands are my best friends;
I like them very much,
If I didn't have hands I wouldn't work at all.
There are hands that start wars.
Some other hand are peace.
My hands will not start war
But will make peace.
They will love the people, poor and sick,
And that's how
All the hands
Of the world
Should be.

Nafisa Parveen (10)
Arden Primary School

OCEANS OF DREAMS

Find the border where the sky meets the sea,
There lies treasure just waiting for me,
Diamonds, emeralds, sapphires, pearls,
All buried in the deep blue sea.

Find the treasure of your dreams,
There it is, much closer than it seems,
Don't give up until it's found,
I'll give you a clue,
It's deep down on the ground.

Alina Iqbal (9)
City Road School

THE DYING DRAGON

In the middle of the mountain,
Inside a cave,
A dusty old dragon,
Heading for his grave.

As cold as snow,
Raging storms overhead,
There is gleaming gold,
That scatter in his bed.

The best of dragons,
There will not be anymore,
And slow beats his heart,
While he is dying on the floor.

At last there will be no more fire,
Like when he did roar,
The best of dragons,
Is breathing no more.

Taimoor Shafiq (9)
City Road School

TWINKLING IN THE SKY

A Milky Way full of stars.
As shiny as glitter.
Small as a dot.
A beautiful constellation.
The sky shining like a diamond.
It makes a beautiful cluster dancing in the sky.
Like a spark of fire.
Wishing on them.

Sumaiyah Khan (10)
City Road School

TIRESOME JOURNEY

All is dark, nothing to see,
The stars whizz past like busy bees
Cotton wool clouds,
Big noisy crowds,
Children rushing, fussing and
Pushing down the narrow aisles.

Here are the air hostesses,
Coming down the line with
Trays of yucky food for us to dine.

What's wrong with Miss Lea?
She looks ravenous,
She's probably missed her tea.

Nearly over,
Journey almost done,
Time to get home and
Have some fun.

Jagbir Kaur (10)
City Road School

POEM

When Betty laughed
She had some tarts
And said she is the
Queen of Hearts.

Nosheen Tabassum (8)
City Road School

THE SEA POEM

The sea is a hungry lion,
It rolls by the beach all day.
One by one, it swallows the fish,
The screeching, screaming sound,
Mumbles inside its tummy.
In June, July and August
The waves calm down.
Hour upon hour it gnaws,
The screeching, screaming sound, it snores.
The storm rushes by,
It wakes up the calm sea.
Anger growls in the large sea's tummy.
The huge sea opens its mouth
And snap, snap it eats another fish.

Ansser Saleem (10)
City Road School

BUTTERFLY POEM

Starting as a caterpillar
Turning into a butterfly
So multicoloured and bright
Flying and zooming through the air
Green like a chrysalis
Red like a fungus
Poisonous flower stings
Yellow like a buttercup
Blue like a bug which has thin striped wings
Feathers on plants blowing and swaying like the wind.

Ambreen Akhtar (9)
City Road School

GRANDAD

Once Grandad was my age
I wonder, when he was eight
Did he smoke a pipe in bed?
On his way to junior school
Did he forget his teeth
And did he use a Zimmer frame
To jog around the house?
Was he ever young?
If so, did he use to pop
Out of the classroom every day
To the pub and betting shop?
Did he chew gum with gums?
Did he scare school bullies?
Simply standing around,
Looking old and smelly?

Fahima (11)
City Road School

SILVER

Silver stars gleaming in the midnight sky,
Silver sweet wrappers gleaming on the midnight streets,
Diamonds glittering like tinsel round a neck of pride,
The silver moon lies proud of its beautiful rays.

Hassan Mahmood (9)
City Road School

WINTER TO AUTUMN

Sleet and snow
As white as dough,

The fierce wind comes raging
Passed our door,

Gloves and scarves,
Slippery paths,

Swelling buds that clutch
A secret treasure,

Gusty winds have chased away and
Squirrels start to play.

Summer has come
Heat pouring from
The golden lips of the sun,

The early morning flowers
Dazzle our eyes,

And now the flowers
Have had all their fun
It's time for them to go,

Brown, red and yellow
Are the leaves and
Bare are the trees,

Dull and dark become the days
For now winter is here once again.

Rahat Hussain (10)
City Road School

UNTITLED

'I cannot go to school today' said little Peggy.
My brains have stopped,
My lungs have flopped.
My bones are rattling,
There's nothing to stop it crackling.
All night I've been eating bones,
I've put on eight stone.
My eyes are blue,
Just like glue.
My legs are long,
I've just learned a song.
My arms are short,
I'm hard to sort.

Mohammed Areeb (8)
City Road School

THE MOON SHINES BRIGHTLY

The gleaming moon lit up the night sky
The moon's happy face made the night shine brightly
The gleaming moon lit up the night sky

The stars sparkle like little moons
The moon shines up high with the stars as its friends
The stars sparkle like little moons

The houses stood still shining in the moon
The moon shone up high making the sky shine beautifully
The houses stood still shining in the moon.

Harriet Scott (8)
Coleshill CE Primary School

NIGHT SKY

Night is flying with dark at its side,
The gloomy dark drowning light,
Greedily gobbling it.

Night is flying with dark at its side,
Shooting stars spreading dust,
The beautiful stars guarding the moon.

Night is flying with dark at its side,
Like a man and his dog
Coming down to Earth.

The night is flying with dark at its side,
But soon the dim night will pass by,
The light will break free
And the sun will rise once more.

Matthew Lloyd (8)
Coleshill CE Primary School

THE NIGHT

The shining moon rose up from the silver fields.
The stars flashing like lightning,
Until the moon lit up the sky.
The owls were swooping past like feathered butterflies.
The rats scampered silently through the long, silver grass.
The glimmer of the stars stroke the moon
Until the glowing moon moved slowly across the sky
And disappeared from the blazing sun.

Lianne Baker (9)
Coleshill CE Primary School

BONFIRE NIGHT

A firework is like a shooting rocket.
A sparkler is like a spitting moon.
The crackling of the bonfire.

A firework is like a shooting rocket.
A sparkler is like a crackling moon.
A firework is like a banging rocket.

A firework is like a shooting rocket.
The spitting and crackling sound of Guy Fawkes burning.

A firework is like a shooting rocket.
A firework is like a banging star.
A Catherine wheel springs in the wind with sparks.

A firework is like a shooting rocket.

Chloe Pudge (8)
Coleshill CE Primary School

THE NIGHT

Moonlight shines everywhere through my window at night.
The gloom glides over my bed looking for a place to go.
Night is dark, it's like a blanket that's covered the world.
Look at the stars in all shapes and sizes,
Twirling and jumping all night long.
Leaves of trees turn silver while the moonlight dazzles.
Leaves fall into rivers and the rivers glow silver.

Rachel Martin (8)
Coleshill CE Primary School

MOONLIGHT

The big, fat moon rising upwards marking
Night has come,
With the man on the moon dancing about
Casting shadows around the Earth.

The little stars like sploshes of glitter
Sparkling one by one,
With moonlight gliding down to Earth,
Lighting up the streets.

The enormous moon shooting beams
In every direction,
Blinding people who shouldn't
Have been watching.

David White (8)
Coleshill CE Primary School

FIREWORKS AND BONFIRES

The grand bonfire lit like a dazzling sun.
A colourful explosion of fireworks
Is like a golden bonfire.
A group of flames blazed powerfully.
The blast of fireworks and fire
Made a bonfire's dinner.
The gleaming glaze of light
Caused the fire to strike the moon at night.
The midnight power invented a bonfire.

Sam Shakespeare (8)
Coleshill CE Primary School

THE FIREWORK DISPLAY

The fireworks have arrived once again,
As we are getting ready to go.

The burning flames light up the night.

The sizzling sparklers sizzle away.

While Guy Fawkes turns to ashes,
And the banging begins.

The bright night is glowing and
So beautifully flashing by the fireworks.

So the taste of candyfloss goes into my mouth
While the pretty fireworks have been let off.

The whizzing rockets fire away,
And the display is burning.

While we all gather around to see the fireworks
So we all end the night with very happy people smiling.

Abby Rose Williams (9)
Coleshill CE Primary School

THE SPARKLING STARS

The moon shone down on the stars lighting up the sky.
People are counting the stars as they go by.
Lighting up their windows, brightening up the sky,
While we enjoy the stars people start to cry.
The stars light up the moonlight glittering as they go.
The dark disappears as the stars begin to glow.

Hannah Coggan (8)
Coleshill CE Primary School

ALIENS

Green and hairy
Super scary

Black dark eyes
Covered in flies

Smelly breath
Completely deaf

Slugs for fingers
And spiky stingers

Scabby toes
Runny nose.

Jordan Hughes (8)
Coleshill CE Primary School

BONFIRE NIGHT

Sparklers shine like shooting stars
Fireworks blast into the air like a blazing rocket
Rockets in the air they rise like fiery flowers
That burst upon the night
A firework is like a light
On bonfires there's woodchips shooting in the air
Fireworks fly like a blasting rocket and
Come down like pieces of Mars
A bonfire makes huge flames from Earth
Sparklers spit like a blazing fire . . .

Jordan Ryan Davies (8)
Coleshill CE Primary School

BONFIRE NIGHT

A bonfire is nice to look at
It shines so nice it lights up the night.

A firework is like a million colourful stars
Shooting over hands.

A Catherine wheel is like a million colours
Blending together.

A bonfire burning, Guy Fawkes crackling.

A firework is standing, it makes a bang in your ear.

A Catherine wheel whizzing around and around.

Laura Young (9)
Coleshill CE Primary School

RIVERS

Rivers sway side to side crashing against the hard jagged rocks.
The wildlife gathered round to take a fresh drink
From the flowing river.
The fish jump and their scales reflect from the bright glowing sun
And twinkle in the deer's eyes.
Now the river is bigger than ever, it says goodbye
To the wildlife and flows into the sea.

Luke Horton (8)
Coleshill CE Primary School

THE ANIMALS OF THE NIGHT

The silver moon's face giggling down on the glittering trees.
Dangling on the branches, in the silent beehives,
Sleep the dreaming bees.
The silver moon's face giggling down on the glittering trees.

The foxes hunting happily,
Dancing on the hills.
The mice scatter helplessly.
The foxes hunting happily,
Dancing on the hills.

The greeny, graceful grass snake,
Slithering like silk.
The waking baby cows cry for their cold milk.
The greeny, graceful grass snake,
Slithering like silk.

The silver moon's face giggling down on the glittering trees.
Dangling on the branches, in the silent beehives,
Sleep the dreaming bees.
The moon's silver face giggling down on the glittering trees,
As midnight draws near.

Victoria Hines-Randle (9)
Coleshill CE Primary School

THE MINOTAUR

The murderous, merciless monster,
Prowling through the labyrinth,
Greedily waiting for his next victim,
Savage and sinister, his eyes flashed fire.

Curtis Riley (9)
Hobmoor Primary School

THE MINOTAUR

The Minotaur,
Half man, half bull,
Stalking through his labyrinth,
Starving for food,
As vicious as a viper,
He loves human flesh,
A cruel, sinister savage,
A merciless menacing monster,
A black horned, brutal beast,
Eyes as hot as a volcano,
But then comes to his death
Which stops his bloodthirstiness . . .
Forever and ever.

Daniel Lenton (9)
Hobmoor Primary School

THE MINOTAUR

A savage and sinister beast
That guards a maze full of mysteries,
His heart is pure evil,
He's a nightmare come true,
Wicked and wrong,
Dangerous and dreadful,
His horns are as sharp as the hunter's knife,
His eyes glow fire,
He's bloodthirsty for his next victim,
The *Minotaur*.

Hannah Scarr (10)
Hobmoor Primary School

I LOVE CATS BECAUSE...

I love cats because they're cute,
I love cats because they're fluffy,
I love cats because they have long tails,
I love cats because they are intelligent,
I love cats because they're beautiful,
I love cats because their ears are cute,
I love cats because they have wet noses,
I love cats because they have lovely eyes,
I love cats because they don't really bite,
I love cats because they have long eyelashes,
I love cats because
They're just cats.

They're just cats.

Chloe Robinson (7)
Hobmoor Primary School

WILD WOOD

The wind was screaming and screeching
It was the sound of howling spectres
The moon was like the Devil's head burning with anger
The wood was an army of spectres
Its floor was like vampires' coffins cold and hard
Thunder was a werewolf gnashing its teeth together
Lightning was the wacky, wicked witches making shocking spells
The clouds were the blood of the evil Frankenstein.

Jake Bett (10)
Hobmoor Primary School

THE ANIMAL SHOW

Hi, my name is Mole,
I've just dug a hole,
I've ate a worm,
Boy, did it squirm,
I didn't even use a bowl.

My name is Kanger,
I come from down under,
I'm hopping mad,
I'm really glad,
That I'm not a panda.

Hello my name is Cheet,
I'm fast on my feet,
I show my jaws
And tremendous claws,
I eat any meat I meet.

Matthew Ashmore (10)
Hobmoor Primary School

THESEUS

Theseus, the brave and daring Theseus
Was determined to kill the vicious killer
Every year, seven boys and seven girls were sent into the labyrinth
As heroic Theseus went down,
He could hear the snuffling of the Minotaur
As it charged, Theseus drew his sword into the bloodthirsty beast
Theseus had tried to kill the Minotaur . . .
. . . and he succeeded.

Steven Wright (10)
Hobmoor Primary School

THE BLITZ

The German planes were big bullies,
Dropping bombs in dark gullies,
The sneakin', spitting, scary machines,
Roaring through the sky,
Are dropping bombs on passers-by,
Buzz, buzz, bang, bang, boom,
A doodlebug is coming soon,
The red glares of the town,
A thundering incendiary has burnt the
Houses down,
As the planes spit out,
People shout
'A doodlebug has just . . .
. . . cut out!'

Zoë Lee (10)
Hobmoor Primary School

THE DONKEY DOO

'What is a donkey doo Daddy?'
'A donkey doo son' said I
'Is a donkey with wings
And it wears a nose ring
And makes a mess with his pie'

'How strange is a donkey doo Daddy?'
'As strange as strange' I replied
'When the king wears his crown,
It jumps up and down
And it's got three nanny goat's eyes.'

Jack Coady (10)
Hobmoor Primary School

THE MINOTAUR

Roaming round for its prey,
Getting ready to pounce on its next victim,
Ferocious, barbaric monster,
The monstrous villain,
The fiendish beast,
The barbarous, brutal murderer,
Sniffling for the smell of human blood,
Pouncing, diving for its prey,
Ripping, tearing flesh.
Waiting for the human,
Who was going to try to stop its bloodthirstyness
Forever.

Lee Merritt (10)
Hobmoor Primary School

THE MINOTAUR

The Minotaur,
Was a cold-blooded beast who lived in a maze,
While roaming round for his prey,
He was the biggest, baddest exterminator around,
Every year eating seven boys and seven girls,
He was a big beast,
Theseus went to slay the Minotaur,
He took a ball of string and a sword,
With one mighty swing he heard
Hack!
The Minotaur was dead.

Christopher Hughes (10)
Hobmoor Primary School

BEN THE DOG

Ben the dog likes to run,
He also likes to sit in the sun,
He likes his food
And sometimes gets in a bad mood,
He's brown and white
And likes to fight,
He's 13 years old,
But always does as he's told.

Ben the dog likes his ball,
But sometimes has a little fall,
He's slightly deaf and old too,
But always likes something new,
At 6pm Ben has his supper,
While my nan has a cuppa,
But now it's night,
So Ben would like to say goodnight
And he snuggles up tight
'Goodnight.'

Emma Sandford (10)
Hobmoor Primary School

THE MINOTAUR

The big-headed, barbaric beast,
Searches the labyrinth for his next victim,
Horns as sharp as a guillotine's blade,
Teeth as pointed as knives,
Rotten bones from the seven boys and
Seven girls spreading a foul stench around the maze.

Dalian Taylor (10)
Hobmoor Primary School

ROBOT WARS

The robots will bash,
House robots will smash,
Chaos2 will flip you
And Firestorm too.

Killalot with his mighty claw,
Will drop them in the pits,
Dead Metal with his super saw,
Will slice them into bits.

There is X-Terminator2 with his axe
And Razer who always whacks,
Matilda with a squeezing jaw,
Will jam and squeeze you to the floor.

Jake Humphries (9)
Hobmoor Primary School

THE MINOTAUR

Evil, mean, savage Minotaur,
His heart pounding,
He stood there,
Waiting for his next victim,
He heard his next victim,
Walking closer and closer,
Until . . .
He pounced.

Sarah Pinfield (9)
Hobmoor Primary School

MY BABY BROTHER

I want my brother to be born,
He's due here any day,
I really wish he'd hurry up,
Then we could start to play.

I've longed to see what he looks like,
I'm sure he'll look just fine,
Will he have short, dark, curly hair
And will it look like mine?

I'll help my mum when he is born
And show her that I care,
By giving him baths and feeds too,
I think that's only fair.

Amy Bryan (9)
Hobmoor Primary School

THE MINOTAUR

As bloodthirsty as a vampire,
Eyes as hot as lava,
His teeth as sharp as razors
And breath smelling like a rotten egg,
He hungers for his next victim,
As he works himself round and round,
The labyrinth,
Waiting . . .
For his prey to appear.

Samantha Morris (10)
Hobmoor Primary School

THE MINOTAUR

The devilish, devious Minotaur lurked in the shadows,
Waiting impatiently for his next victim,
The big, brutal bully waited for the smell of humans,
His feet were as heavy as lead
And his vile, ugly, foul smelling body,
Filled the labyrinth with a horrible stench.

Amy Quinn (9)
Hobmoor Primary School

THE MINOTAUR

The big, barbaric beast,
Stomped up and down the labyrinth's tunnels,
His foul smell racing round every corner,
While waiting for the taste of human flesh.

A barbaric beast,
A merciless, murderous menace,
A sinister, sadistic, savage bully.

Katie Bateman (9)
Hobmoor Primary School

THUNDER AND LIGHTNING

Thunder and lightning is so frightening,
You lie awake and start to shake,
You open your eyes to the sound of the noise,
With a flash I hear a crash.
I jump on the floor and run to the door,
Thunder and lightning is so frightening.

Kirsten Smith (10)
Hobmoor Primary School

THE MINOTAUR

Eyes as red as fire,
A vile killer,
Hungry!
Waiting for his next fourteen children,
Black-hearted,
Teeth as sharp as thorns,
Cold-blooded as a shark.

Jade Foster (9)
Hobmoor Primary School

MARY ROSE

I was standing on board Mary Rose
Hundreds of people were on board,
King Henry was waving good luck,
We set sail immediately.

We were not far from land,
I heard a creaking noise,
The ship sank, I drowned,
Then . . . I closed my eyes, I had died!

Natalie Reynolds (9)
Hobmoor Primary School

I KNOW A LADY WITH A CAT

I know a lady with a cat
And Chelsey is her name,
We go to see her once a week
And play lots of games.

Paris Cairns (10)
Hobmoor Primary School

DREAMS

Dreams are lovely,
When you're flying in the sky and talking to animals,
When you're also breathing under the sea,
Even when you're a mermaid swimming in the sea with the fish.

But . . .
Dreams can be nightmares,
You might be chased by monsters,
Or you cannot breath under the sea,
But don't worry you'll wake up.

When you get to the end of a good dream
And you want to know what's going to happen next,
Sadly you wake up and don't know what might of
Happened at the end of that beautiful dream.
Luckily the weekend approaches and you get a longer sleep.

Matthew Murphy (10)
Hobmoor Primary School

MY PET SNAKE

I have a pet snake,
His name is Jake,
He slithers about on the floor.

He has big eyes,
He eats meat pies
And then he shows his big jaw.

My pet snake is very nice,
I got him for a cheap price.

Connor Ashmore (7)
Hobmoor Primary School

NATURE

The birds, the bees,
The flowers, the trees,
They all grow up together.
The quickness of the birds and bees,
Flying in the heather.
The beauty of the flowers and trees
Growing in the grass.
Always take a look at them,
Any time you pass.

But don't just focus on those,
They're other things around,
There's toadstools
And mushrooms,
Which grow on the ground.
But mind where you step,
'Cause there's fairies
In the grass.
Always take a look at them,
Any time you pass.

Kirsty Merritt (10)
Hobmoor Primary School

MY BEST MATE

Becky is my best mate
And I am her best friend Kate,
We are best friends
And she always says
We are best mates
And she loves to paint.

Katy Leek (7)
Hobmoor Primary School

THE EGG AND ME

The egg and me
Went for tea,
His name is Irfan
And he is from Japan.
He's friends with Britney Spears,
He said that he pulled her out of his ears,
I knew he was lying,
But soon he'll be frying.
I cracked him into the pane
And he changed his name to Dan.
By this time, he was done,
So I slammed him into a bun.
I took a bottle of Sprite
Then took a bite,
So that was the end of Dan,
Who was from Japan!

Faaria Hussain (10)
Hobmoor Primary School

MOM'S OLD CAR AND THE RESCUE MAN

Mom's old car didn't go far,
One day we went to the seaside, where the engine died.
Thank goodness for the rescue man and his yellow van.
One day we went to the safari park where we were
Stuck there till it was dark.
Thank goodness for the rescue man in the yellow van.
We finally got a brand new car that went far,
The only thing is I miss my rescue man and his yellow van.

Luke Scarr (8)
Hobmoor Primary School

TROPICAL ISLAND

Tropical island, tropical island,
See all the coconut trees,
Dig in the sand, dig in the sand,
Find the treasure, to be grand.

Tropical island, tropical island,
See all the fish,
Swim from the shark, swim from the shark,
Go to the surfers, it's too dark.

Tropical island, tropical island,
Leaves are green, leaves are green,
Let's make it shine and shine.

Katrina Coleman (7)
Hobmoor Primary School

MIDNIGHT

Midnight moves silent in the night,
Making sure he's out of sight,
He sneaks around as quiet as a mouse
And sometimes looks inside your house.

He rummages through our dusty bin,
To see what he will find within,
He sips a drink in the rain water puddle
And slips in the rain and gets in a muddle.

For his den, he finds a box
He of course, is a sleepy fox.

Melissa Pattison (11)
Hobmoor Primary School

MY TREASURES

First there's Mum, she sings and hums,
Next is Chris, he likes lots of tropical fish,
Jake started nursery when he was only three, he cried
All the time because he missed his mommy.
It ends happily cos he made lots of friends,
Lastly there's Aunty Bev, she loves
History, Mom, Jake, Chris and me.

These are my treasures, my pleasures, my family!

Gemma Webb (9)
Hobmoor Primary School

YOUR SMILES

A gun can kill,
Wind can chill,
Fire can burn,
The mind can learn,
Anger can rage until it
Tears you apart,
But the power of your smile
Melts my heart.

Christopher Dyson (10)
Hobmoor Primary School

THE BLITZ

Crash, crash, boom, boom, boom,
The German bombers are coming soon,
Sirens sounding, fiery sky,
Hear the bombs buzzing by,
The fear, the smell, fire burning,
Inside of me, my heart is churning.

Look out of the shelter on a red-hot night,
Stare up at the sky, see a dogfight,
Hear a person loudly shout, hear the warning,
Time for blackout.
Now they're going, zooming away,
'I know the Blitz is here to stay!'

Jenny Macken (11)
Hobmoor Primary School

'DAD CAN I WATCH THE FOOTIE?'

'Dad can I watch the footie?'
'No your sister's watching Sooty,'
'Don't you want to watch Man U?'
'Hang on I need the loo.'
'Don't you want to watch Beckham and Keane?'
'No Keane's far to mean.'
'OK can I check the score?'
'Well I do agree Sooty is a bore.'
'I'll just put on ITV,'
'Move over son, I can't see!'

Daniel Carroll (11)
Hobmoor Primary School

WAR

Bombs are snapping viciously,
Planes roaring in the sky.
Shelters are rumbling like hungry monsters,
While there is a dogfight nearby,
Doodlebugs whining in the sky
Until . . . they fall.

Sian Phillips (10)
Hobmoor Primary School

MY DAD'S HIDDEN TREASURES

He thinks they're the best,
He says they're better than all the rest,
All he's got is this old car,
It goes 'Bang, bang' all down the road,
I am even embarrassed to go to school,
He tells my mates awful jokes,
When he goes my
Teacher says 'Don't talk to strangers!'
All I have to say is
My dad is . . .

Please say at home and keep your nose out!

Jake Dolphin (10)
Hobmoor Primary School

THE BLITZ

Watching planes flying by,
Black angels of death in the sky.
Screaming and shouting you hear
And planes coming, far and near.
Down into the shelter we run,
With Mum screaming 'Come on son!'
As the planes crash, they crackle and clatter,
A deaf lady asks 'What is the matter?'
The sirens screech louder and louder,
As the sky becomes full of gunpowder.
Black smoke billows up and away,
We get the all-clear next day.

Claire Leek (10)
Hobmoor Primary School

ROBOT WARS

Roboteers stand by,
The house robots never die,
Razer will immobilise,
George Francis drives wise.
Killalot will smash you to bits,
Then he will put you in the pit.
Chaos2 will flip you down,
Shunt will knock you to the ground.
Hipnodisc will whack you hard,
Firestorm will flip you a yard
And if you want to have a bash,
See Robot Wars and watch them smash.

Adam Humphries (8)
Hobmoor Primary School

THE SNAGON

It slithers along the undergrowth
Then rears up tall as big as a boat.
It hisses and roars
And scratches its claws,
Then zooms into the air.
It's out to scare.
If you see its fiery-red eyes,
You'd better run, you'd better hide
It's hungry for food,
And wants you stewed
But you're too late
The Snagon has found you.

Alex Dealaselle (9)
Lickey Hills Primary School

SCHOOL

Some teachers are big
Some are small,
I mind about their sizes
Not at all.

My school is cool
If you're no fool,
Maths is a blast
History's the past.

The children are noisy
The teachers get cross,
Homework's abandoned
But that's no loss.

Games is fun
Especially in the sun,
Sports day's a pleasure
That's what I treasure.

Some people are mean
That's not all I've seen,
But art's the best
Better than all the rest!

Naomi Byatt (8)
Lickey Hills Primary School

THE GIRABEAR

The Girabear is
Faster than a motorbike speeding
Round a track
Taller than a giraffe with a stretched neck

Funnier than a circus clown
Brighter than a spotlight
Softer than a sponge cake
The Girabear.

Ben Wiggett (9)
Lickey Hills Primary School

READING

Oh no,
It's that day again,
I wish I was absent,
Reading gives me pain,

I can't escape,
The teacher is calling my group,
I slowly get up,
With my head in a loop,

Oh good,
I'm going last,
I wait quietly,
While the time goes past,

My turn,
I'm very sad,
I read my page and think,
That wasn't so bad,

But . . .

I'm in pain
It's that day again!

Emily Worthing (8)
Lickey Hills Primary School

CITY SOUND

I like sound

The roar of the train
The rush of the wind
The loud boom of thunder
The zoom of the cars
The tick and the tock of the city clock
The bark of the dog as it chases the cat
The cat goes miaow, miaow, miaow
In the dark of the night
I had such a fright
I scream with terror and fright
Standing in a patch of bright moonlight.

Maria Wesbury (11)
Lickey Hills Primary School

THE MICE

Little mice, little mice
So small and so tiny
Will you come out to play today?

Little mice, little mice
So grey and so pink ears
Will you come out to play today?

Little mice, little mice
So fun and so happy
Will you come out to play today?

Charlotte Juggins (8)
Lickey Hills Primary School

A Day In The Life Of Flipper

Flipper wakes up,
Splashes
Finds a place on the seabed
He rests
Plays with his younger brother
And sleeps
Flipper wakes up
Splashes
Inspects the seabed
Finds a place to rest
And sleeps
Flipper wakes up
Comes under shelter
Inspects the rocks
Gets the crabs to chase him
And sleeps
Dreaming of his busy day *zzzzz.*

Emma Gardiner (8)
Lickey Hills Primary School

The Wehttam

The Wehttam is
Slower than an overweight snail,
Fluffier than a baby chick,
Quieter than a butterfly,
Whiter than a summer cloud,
More pleasant than daffodils.
The Wehttam.

Matthew Kings (8)
Lickey Hills Primary School

MY PETS

In my bathroom
I keep
Ten tortoises that tickle their tummies,
Nine newts that nibble their nails,
Eight elephants with ever so hairy legs,
Seven snakes that slither and slide,
Six sabre-toothed tigers that spring about,
Five foxes that fly,
Four fish that float in the bath,
Three throstles that are thirsty,
Two turtles that play the trumpet,
And *one* . . .
Boy in the bath - me!

Thomas Hubscher (8)
Lickey Hills Primary School

THE CROCRAB

The Crocrab is:
Bigger than ten fat horses
Slower than a slug on a rocky path
Sillier than two thousand clowns put together
Browner than a mud-covered pig
Shorter than a pencil snapped in half
Hungrier than nine thousand thin pigs
More beautiful than seven hundred peacocks
More intelligent than five hundred head teachers
The Crocrab.

Tina Wesbury (8)
Lickey Hills Primary School

In My Bathroom

In my bathroom I had
Ten jumping frogs
Nine crawling caterpillars
Eight slithering snakes
Seven spiky hedgehogs
Six roaring lions
Five scattered cockroaches
Four barking dogs
Three eight-legged spiders
Two buckled bugs
One annoying *sister*
In my bathroom.

Luke Clarke (8)
Lickey Hills Primary School

Tom's Pets

In my garden I keep:
Ten blue whales that throw me up in the air,
Nine black cranes that have long beaks,
Eight giraffes that have blue tongues,
Seven sharks who have just been eaten,
Six goldfish that were in with the sharks,
Five eagles that fly in the air,
Four monkeys that are having a cup of tea,
Three donkeys that kick,
Two cats that have huge teeth
And one boy who is going *crazy!*

Tom Brazil (8)
Lickey Hills Primary School

LOUIS THE LITTLE

He tipped custard in PC Clark's helmet - red peppers in Bowser's
dog bowl . . .
(He leapt right up on the pelmet, with smoke pouring from his earhole!)
Shoved compost in Grandfather's welly and spiders in
Grandma's cocoa . . .
Old Gramps' foot got dreadfully smelly - and Granny went totally loco!
Put glue in his mum's frilly knickers and fleas in his dear dad's vest -
He also put some in the vicar's (to see who could disco dance best!)
He loves putting things in the wrong places - I would say that it fills
him
with glee,
As he looks at his poor victims' faces, he says:
'Guess where they would like to put me?'

Michael Harrison (9)
Lickey Hills Primary School

MY CAT

I bought myself a cat,
It turned into a rat.
The rat ate a bat,
That was my dainty cat.
When it turned back,
It turned into a rabbit.
That rabbit,
That rabbit
Had a very bad habit!
That was my dainty rabbit.

Bradley Styring (8)
Lickey Hills Primary School

FAREWELL GOOD FRIEND

When I look at the stars I see your face,
Smiling as it used to,
But it becomes so blurred for I am crying.
I turn away from your tender warmth,
Remembering how I looked deep into your eyes.
You were my home, my den and my place
You took me out on winter walks,
I was happy, but now you are gone.
I hear your name when the wind blows,
Calling,
Longing.
I remember your laugh, like music to my ears,
But you cannot laugh any longer.
I sit here enveloped in bereavement.
I am heartbroken, it is true,
Because my life is not the same without you.

'Why did you go?' I ask,
'And why did it happen so soon?
Tell me, why did you leave me in such pain?'
All these questions I have to know,
But the stars in the night sky,
The wind in my ears, tell me something important.
I am *not* worthless without you,
I have to be strong, not emotional, not too long.
Even though I love you so and miss you dearly,
Life *will* go on for me.
When I look at the stars above,
I see your face smiling,
Smiling down at me,
Comforting me, all the time.

Hollie Brader (9)
Lickey Hills Primary School

MISS AND SIR

'Miss, John hit me,
Miss, I'm stuck,
Miss, I need the toilet,
Miss, how do you spell *because?*

Miss! . . .'

'Sir, Paul hit me,
Sir, I'm stuck,
Sir, I need the toilet,
Sir, how do you spell *because?*

Sir! . . .'

'John do your work,
John go outside,
John go to the head
(And don't come back)

John . . .'

'Paul do your work,
Paul go outside,
Paul go to the head
(And don't come back)

Paul . . .'

Peter Jennens (10)
Osborne J&I School

JACK

That clean man called Jack,
He lives on sticky chocs,
He keeps chocolate in his socks,
He even licks his shoes,
That sticky man called Jack!

That sticky man called Jack,
Gets paid a tenner a week,
With a sticky little cheek,
He plays hide-and-seek,
That sticky man called Jack.

Kim Harris (10)
Osborne J&I School

ABOUT MY FAMILY

My uncle Dan likes
To eat jam.

My sister loves to
Eat pizza.

My dog Boots loves
To eat fruits.

My cousin Sandy
Loves to drink brandy.

My sweet mom
Always fills my tum.

My dad is always mad.

My auntie Gillian
Is one in a million.

I love my family
More than anything
In the world.

My family is the
Best family in the world.

Victoria Watts (10)
Osborne J&I School

BOOKS

Some are good
Some are bad
Some are sad
Some are mad

Some are big
Some are small
Some are light
Some are heavy

Some have words
Some have pictures
Some have both
Some have none

Most have authors
Most have illustrators
Some are easy
Some are hard

Happy ending
Nasty ending
Good ending
Bad ending.

Thomas Allen (10)
Osborne J&I School

EPITAPHS

Here lies the body of David Jones
Who fell from a building
And broke his bones,
Nobody knows how he died,
Many thought it was suicide.

Here lies the body of Mrs Peer,
Who sat for hours,
In her rocking chair,
She rocked herself to the Land of Nod
And now she rocks in Heaven with God.

Jason Lakin (10)
Osborne J&I School

MY DOG JESSIE

My dog Jessie is six years old,
Never does what she is told,
My dog Jessie is really cute,
My dog Jessie is not a brute.
My dog Jessie, she loves to play,
She is forever here to stay.
I love you a lot Jessie,
Even though you're really messy,
You chase the cat,
You chase the rat,
You're not perfect, I know,
But everyone loves your collar that glows
And when I got Brian the dog,
My dad said, 'You big, fat hog'
And when little Snowballs came,
We had to hold you with a cane,
Then came Scabbers the rat,
You chased it more than you chased the cat
And if you ever pull the plug,
It's your own fault for eating a slug.

Natalie Bates (10)
Osborne J&I School

DOGS

Dogs big, dogs small,
Dogs short, dogs tall,
Dogs fat, dogs thin,
Dogs that make a dreadful din.

Dogs smooth, dogs hairy,
Dogs friendly, dogs scary,
Dogs brown, dogs white,
Dogs that bark all through the night.

Dogs that run, dogs that walk,
Dogs that make you think they'll talk,
Dogs awake, dogs asleep,
Dogs for the blind, dogs for the sheep.

The best of all the dogs I know,
Goes with me everywhere I go.

Sarish Akhtar (10)
Osborne J&I School

A HUNTER

A hunter is keen,
A hunter is mean,
A hunter eats meat,
A hunter takes a seat,
A hunter has fur,
A hunter has a purr.

A catalogue to make the hunter a lion.

Alisha Gordon (10)
Osborne J&I School

SNOWFLAKES

Snowflakes,
Snowflakes,
All around.

Snowflakes,
Snowflakes,
On the ground.

Snowflakes,
Snowflakes,
Make it bright.

Snowflakes,
Snowflakes,
Make a lovely sight.

Francesca Heath (10)
Osborne J&I School

SUMMER'S HERE

Look, the freezing ice cream's
Running down your hand.
Look, the cheerful children playing on the sand.
The glimmering sea splashing against the shore.
Look, the playful ponies playing in the moor.
Look, the baby rabbits just starting to hop.
Look, the thirsty people queuing at the shop.
Look, the dancing sunflowers swaying in the breeze.
Look, the hungry seagulls eating bread and cheese.

Jacqueline Meeley (11)
Osborne J&I School

QUEEN'S JUBILEE

It's the Queen's Jubilee,
A time full of glee,
It's on June the 3rd,
So go and spread the word.

There'll be parties in the street,
For everyone to meet,
So come along
And party all night long,
Pay a small fee and celebrate the
Queen's
Jubilee.

Nadine Brittle (11)
Osborne J&I School

SPACE

Space is a deep black hole,
That never ever ends,
The sun that shines,
To give us day,
Space never ends,
Strange and weird planets
Out there,
No one knows them,
Space that never,
Space that never.
Space that never ends.

Samantha Ames (12)
Osborne J&I School

MY SPECIAL TREAT

My favourite dessert is a knickerbocker glory,
It's all done in sections, a bit like a story,
It's got a lovely beginning, a middle and an end,
I save all my money, so on Saturday I can spend
All my cash on a treat just for me,
It gets my taste buds all in a twist,
The colours and flavours are an endless list,
Vanilla ice cream and chocolate chip,
Hundreds and thousands stuck to my lip,
Chopped nuts, coconut, brandy snaps too,
A knickerbocker glory is a dream come true.
The strawberries sweet, the bananas yummy,
All of the tastes mixed up in my tummy,
Roll on Saturday when my money I can spend,
Down at the coffee shop with my best friend.

Trudie Collins (11)
Osborne J&I School

WHAT A GAME

Leeds versus Villa,
What a thriller,
Rushing up and down the pitch,
Even though they have a stitch,
Villa have scored, what a killer,
The goal scorer was
Young Thomas Miller.

Michael O'Cleary (10)
Osborne J&I School

APRIL CINQUAIN

April
Flowers are formed,
Green leaves are on the trees,
Birds are tweeting along a song,
April.

April
Beach sand sparkles
Sea sand crumbles in hand
See the sea, sand and things around
April.

April
People away
To see the sites today,
Traffic jams in their caravans
April.

Emily Yarnold (10)
Osborne J&I School

AT THE BEACH

At the beach, there's golden sand,
Sunbathers are all tanned,
When the waves came the children ran,
People are drinking from a Pepsi can,
The boats are sailing on the sea,
Carrying people on a long journey.

Stacey Ames (11)
Osborne J&I School

THERE'S A GHOST IN OUR SCHOOL LIBRARY

There's a ghost in our school library,
None of the teachers care.
Even though the ghost
Messes up their hair
They say it's just the wind,
We know it isn't that.
Who else could it be?
The caretaker's cat!
The ghost brings chaos
And disorder
To alphabetical order.
The teachers blame the kids
They can't see further than their eyelids,
There's a ghost in our school library
And we don't know what to do
Who can help us?
Will it be you?

Charlotte Tooze (10)
Osborne J&I School

HOPE

Hope can be found in a pure child's eyes,
In your souls, that's where it lies.
Close your mind, go deep within
Let it be free!
Because if you do you're certain to win,
Hope can be found inside you!

Lauren Hartill (10)
Osborne J&I School

THERE WAS A YOUNG MAN FROM DUNDEE

There was a young man from Dundee,
Whose favourite drink was tea,
One day he tried Coke
And got totally broke,
That silly young man from Dundee.

Edmund van der Molen (11)
Osborne J&I School

WINTER

Look, the glistening nail on the roof,
Look, the transparent rocket from the sky,
Look, the feathery pillow on the floor,
Look, the shimmering marbles from the sky,
Look, the gloomy smoke in the sky,
Look, the rustling leaves rusting on the floor.

Halima Javid (11)
Osborne J&I School

THE MAN FROM CALCUTTA

There was a man from Calcutta,
Who always talked with a stutter,
As thin as a stick,
Could not pick a brick
And always slipped through the gutter.

Aleema Akhter (11)
Osborne J&I School

THE SUN

I can make people happy by giving them a tan,
I can make people sad by burning them,
I can make people play and go to the park,
I can make people laugh and have a good joke,
I can make people look funny by making them red,
I can make people swim in their pool.

Kadie O'Loughlin (11)
Osborne J&I School

THE TRAMP ON A PIER

There was an old tramp on a pier,
Who loved cigarettes and beer,
He opened his bag,
Pulled out a fag,
The dirty old tramp on a pier.

Jake Malkin (11)
Osborne J&I School

THE DRUNK MAN ON THE TOP BUNK

There was a man who was drunk
Who slept on the top bunk,
He fell on the floor
And hit his head on the door
That injured man who was drunk.

Charlie Prosser (10)
Osborne J&I School

NAMES!

A is for Aaron who drank a lot of Coke,
B is for Ben who tells lots of jokes,
C is for Chantel who flew to the stars,
D is for Danisha who's never seen Mars,
E is for Edmund who jumped in a pond,
F is for Frank who's got a magic wand,
G is for Gemma who's reading a story,
H is for Harna who wants praise and glory,
I is for Ian who wants lots of money,
J is for Jake who goes out when it's sunny,
K is for Kane who loves chips and jelly,
L is for Lizzy who's socks are smelly,
M is for Mary who's quite contrary,
N is for Naomi who's never weary,
O is for Oliver who drinks out of a can,
P is for Peter who's called Peter Pan,
Q is for Quentin who always moans,
R is for Rebecca who talks on the phone,
S is for Samantha who chats all the time,
T is for Thomas who can't read a sign,
U is for Ursula who fell off a swing,
V is for Victoria who doesn't know a thing,
W is for William who's got a cat,
X is for Xzena who slipped on a mat,
Y is for Yvonne who watches TV all day,
Z is for Zoe who doesn't know her way.

Danisha Clarke (10)
Osborne J&I School

NAMES

A for Aaron who loves transport
B for Ben who likes chicks and hens
C is for Cat who likes Pat
D is for Daniel who is a spaniel
E is for Eddy who watches Ed and Eddy
F is for Frank who swam then sank
G is for Gemma who watches TV
H is for Harna who eats banana
I is for Ivan who eats beans
J is for Jake who's like a rake
K is for Kevin who likes red herring
L is for Lisa who likes pizza
M is for Michelle who likes Hell
N is for Nathan who like egg and bacon
O is for Owen who likes poems
P is for Paul who likes to be cool
Q is for the Queen who likes to be mean
R is for Rachel who hates you
S is for Scott who likes spots
T is for Trevor who likes it whenever
U is for Ursula who likes cute purses
V is for Vicky who likes being picky
W is for Wendy who likes being trendy
X is for Xena who likes being keener
Y is for Yvonne who likes being lonely
Z is for Zach who likes a pack.

Zach Jones
Osborne J&I School

SID

Sid the silent, sneaky snake,
Couldn't even bake a cake.

He slithered to the village race,
It started, it was a great pace.

He was first,
Another one burst.

They all passed,
He was last.

He slid off home
He felt all alone.

Ben Greenway (10)
Osborne J&I School

As, As, As

As keen as mustard, with ambition,
As red as beetroot, covered in blood,
As stubborn as a legless mule, who ran out of fuel,
As sour as vinegar, mixed with lemon,
As wise as an owl, who has gone on the prowl,
As green as grass, hard as brass,
As dry as dust, just like blood lust,
As sick as a dog, heavy as a hog,
How white is snow? We'll never know,
How swift is an arrow? See you tomorrow!

Kieran Vauls (10)
Osborne J&I School

THE CLASSROOM

There was chaos in the classroom,
The children couldn't care less
When the teacher walked through the door,
The classroom was a mess,
Mr Neills was his name,
Killing kids was his game,
Slowly and quietly
Katie got out from the line,
Sticking a bomb down his pants
And blowing off his behind.
When Mrs Nevil walked through the door,
There was a grenade lying on the floor,
She stepped on it, had a fit,
Now she is dead on the floor.

Jenna Robbins (10)
Osborne J&I School

I HATE SCHOOL

I hate getting up in the morning to come to school,
I only like Tuesday when we go to the swimming pool,
I hate Mondays when we've got a whole week ahead,
Every boring school day, I just want to stay in bed,
So when the teacher says I'm late,
I'll let the cat out of the bag and say she's got a date.
All the class will shout and scream,
I'd have ruined the teacher's dream.

Elizabeth Wibby (11)
Osborne J&I School

FLYING HIGH

Flying high,
Flying high,
Flying low,
Flying low.

Flying in the middle,
Flying in the middle,
Flying three-quarter high,
Flying three-quarter high,
Flying halfway,
Flying halfway,
Flying one quarter high,
Flying one quarter high,
Flying at the top,
Flying at the top.

Dean Cox (10)
Osborne J&I School

LIVERPOOL

Gerrard passes to young Owen,
The defenders don't know where he's going,
He has a shot from long range,
It's hit a player and the ball has changed
Goal! Liverpool have scored,
The away fans are really bored.

Thomas Cox (10)
Osborne J&I School

SCHOOL

School, school is so cool
Pupils learning teachers' rule
Maths is boring spelling more
School, school is so cool
I wish there was a swimming pool
A big hall, teachers are the best
School, school is so cool
Someone acting like a fool
Many people playing in class
Miss is getting more mad
One boy's even sad
All I want is a DVD just for me
Mind you it's a school
They don't give you everything!

Ross Harrison (9)
Osborne J&I School

THE DINOSAUR AND THE MINOTAUR

There was a dinosaur
And there was a minotaur.
They had lots of fun
Until they saw a nun
And gobbled her up in one go.

Adel Horton (10)
Osborne J&I School

A FRIEND!

She is nice and fun,
She's hot as spice,
She laughs and runs,
When she's not here, she's not fun,
When she's here, it's a lot of fun.

You're really special and good,
You're not like heavy metal,
You're always fun and joyful,
If someone hurt you, don't walk away,
You walk up and say 'Are you OK?'
Because you're the best ever friend!
Best friend forever!

Stephanie Jefferies (10)
Osborne J&I School

THERE'S A MONSTER IN . . .

There's a monster in the classroom
I don't know what to do.
There's a monster in the classroom
He's hiding behind you!
There's a monster in the classroom
Who's swimming in the pool.
There's a monster in the classroom
Who's being such a fool.
There's a monster in the classroom
It really isn't fair.
There's a monster in the classroom
The teacher isn't scared!

Kirstie Waldron (10)
Osborne J&I School

MISS STATHAM

Miss Statham
Up in the sky.

Miss Statham
Can we fly?

Miss Statham
Don't be scared of the dark.

Miss Statham,
Don't bark.

Miss Statham,
Where's Dad?

Miss Statham's sad.

Rebekah Statham (10)
Osborne J&I School

COLOURS OF THE RAINBOW!

Colours of the rainbow,
Red, pink, blue, yellow.

Colours of the rain,
Red, pink, blue down the drain!

Colours of the bow,
Blue, yellow and gold.

Colours of the rainbow.

Michila Jarrett (9)
Osborne J&I School

A POEM FOR AMERICA

September the 11th
Nobody would expect
For terror to arrive
Into their pleasant country America.

The planes came crashing down
Into the wonderful Twin Towers
But who would do such a thing?
The mystery is yet unsolved.

Washington was in danger too
Another plane had crashed
Into yet another wonderful building.

The Pentagon this was
A five-sided building
Everyone was in shock
Three planes in one day.

New York and then Washington
Two and then one
Just ruins left now
Of those amazing buildings.

The finger was pointed
At Osama bin Laden
He must have wanted war.

He got just what he wanted
I wonder if he is pleased?
Millions of people
Representing their country.

This will never be forgotten
We will always look back
Just think of those poor children
Without any mums or dads.

Kirsty Reading (11)
Paganel Junior School

MY BIRTHDAY

When it is my birthday
I jump around like a kangaroo
I love to have presents
And lots of money too!

When it is my birthday
I play with my new stuff
I play for hours and hours
With my new pink powder puff.

When it is my birthday
I always have a cake
With lots of candles and blue icing
It looks just like an icy lake.

When it is my birthday
And it is time to sleep
I'm tired from all my jumping about
And running on my feet.

Zoe Lakin (11)
Paganel Junior School

DOWN BELOW THE OCEAN . . .

Down below the ocean
I met a fish called Jill
'Come and join me now,' she shouted
'I'll help pay the bill.'

Down below the ocean
I met a fish called Fred
'Get away from here,' he called
'I'm going to chop off your head!'

Down below the ocean
I met a fish called Jane
'Come and have some tea,' she whispered
'Do you live in the lane?'

Lee Witherford (8)
Paganel Junior School

THE MOON

The moon glistens
Like the ashes of a burning bonfire
Floats,
Like a relaxed kite on a sandy beach
Glimmers,
Like the paint on a brand new bike.
Twinkles
Like the lights on a Christmas tree,
Gleams,
Like a wolf's dazzling eyes.
Blazes
Like a sparkling firefly.

Jake Davies (10)
Paganel Junior School

WHAT IS THE SUN . . ?

The sun is a yellow daffodil
Growing from its stalk
It is a yellow fireball
Falling from the heavens.

The sun is a bright banana
Floating in the sky
It is a light bulb lit up
Glowing in a lampshade.

The sun is an orange wine gum
Rolling out of the packet
It is a yellow football
Being kicked out of the stadium.

The sun is a shiny penny
Rolling down the drain
It is a shooting star
Falling from the sky.

The sun is a fireman's hat
Being worn on someone's head
It is a yellow bowling ball
Rattling in the bag.

Rebecca Bradbury (8)
Paganel Junior School

UP BEHIND THE OCEAN . . .

Up behind the ocean
I met a whale called Fred
'Come and join me now,' he whispered.

Guiseppe Carieri (8)
Paganel Junior School

YOU THINK

You think you're really good
But actually quite sad
You never eat your vegetables
It's really quite so bad

You're always drinking cola
And now you do not like it
So now you're drinking soda
It is the weakest drink.

You've gone off in a sulk
So teacher tells you off
You ask your mum to stay at home
Because you've got a cough

You think you're very clever
For eating many sweets
So now your mouth is yellow
You better brush your teeth

It's the end of school
You're going to a party
You don't know what to wear
How about a nightie?

Stephanie Henry (10)
Paganel Junior School

UP ABOVE THE ROOFTOPS ...

Up above the rooftops
I met a bird called Sid
'Would you like a cake,' he screeched
'Or I could give it to a kid.'

Toni Hill (8)
Paganel Junior School

CAN A DOG . . .

Can a dog eat a frog
Standing on his hand?
Can a carrot eat a parrot
On the golden sand?
Can a mouse juggle a house
Standing on his nose?
Can a dove give a shove
While eating a big rose?
Can a fox eat Goldilocks
While standing on his head?
Can a bat wear a hat
While sitting in his bed?
Can a cow give a bow
On a perch?
Can a horse run the course
At the local church?
In all answers to these
You see it's plainly clear
That animals can do such things
Including licking ears.

Holly Clayton (8)
Paganel Junior School

WHO WANTS A CAT LIKE THAT?

There was a young woman called Pat,
Who had a very mad cat.
He walked into the wall,
Then fell into the pool.
Who needs a cat like that?

Samantha Fry (10)
Paganel Junior School

THE SUN IS . . .

The sun is a yellow marigold
Blowing in the breeze
It is a shiny penny
Skipping down the drain.

The sun is a yellow tennis ball
Gliding out into space
It is a yellow golf ball
Bouncing off the green.

The sun is a slippy banana
Lying on the ground
It is a yellow basketball
Bouncing off the ground.

The sun is a yellow air freshener
Sitting on the table
It is a yellow wine gum
Chewed by a fluffy dog.

Lisa McCusker (8)
Paganel Junior School

MY DAD

My dad is great he is my best mate,
We always have lots of fun
We laugh and shout while mucking about
Just to annoy my mom,

With a great big hug and a really sloppy kiss
You just can't miss,
His lovely, happy face.

Katie Rose (9)
Paganel Junior School

MY MOM

My mom is the greatest,
My mom is the bomb,
My mom is the best,
That's why she is my mom.
She is Super Woman, Cat Woman and Super Mom put together.
But better,
Her hair smells of fresh apples,
She is a white dove flying high in the sky,
She looks like a big, juicy, red heart,
That fills me with love.
My mom is the greatest,
My mom is the bomb,
My mom is the best,
My mom is number one,
That's all from my mom.

Maxine Quayle (10)
Paganel Junior School

BUMBLEBEE

Me I am a bumblebee,
Buzzing around the apple tree.

Hovering about collecting nectar,
My furry body which is my protector.

See-through wings and stripy body,
Not wanting to trouble anybody.

I'll sting you if you make me mad,
But really I am not too bad.

Stacie Genders (11)
Paganel Junior School

THE SECRET SPELL

Double, trouble I'm in a muddle
Fire flicker and pot bubble

Weasel's whiskers and cat's blisters
A dog's tail and a monkey's sister
Chunks of horn and samples of cheese
A little more coffee if you please

Milk of cow and wing of flea
Silk of worm and stripe of bee
Snout of pig and eye of rat
Tail of mice and nose of bat

For a spell of comic trouble
Like a lovely broth cackle and double.

Laura Hoult (11)
Paganel Junior School

ANIMAL CRUELTY

Animal cruelty is wrong
It has gone on too long
Why won't it stop?
It scares the animals a lot
And it hurts them too.
So if this is you . . .
Stop and *think*
If it is right.

Kate Robinson (9)
Paganel Junior School

WHEN EMMA WAS A LITTLE GIRL

When Emma was a little girl of one or two or three
She thought it would be nice to be a little bumblebee
She'd buzz around the field all day
And sit inside the flowers
And sip the nectar bit by bit for hours and hours and hours.

When Emma was a bigger girl of four or five or six
She didn't want to be a bee
But learned some other tricks
She stayed around the house all day and drove her mother wild
Who said, 'You're better as a little bee and not a horrid child.'

Emma Wakelin (10)
Paganel Junior School

MY DOG WOOF

My dog Woof
Is too rough,
I sit in the chair
And he's always there,
Pulling my slippers off!

When I walk Woof
Because he's so rough,
He drags me along
All day long,
Wagging his tail behind him!

Laura Pollard (11)
Paganel Junior School

MY MOM

My mom is kind
My mom is boring sometimes
My mom is lovely
My mom is always on the PlayStation
My mom always loves me.

Kelly Gillam (9)
Paganel Junior School

ODDBALL THE DALMATIAN

Oddball the Dalmatian,
Likes going for walks,
Oddball the Dalmatian,
Likes playing ball and catch.

Oddball the Dalmatian,
Sleeps with his owner,
Oddball the Dalmatian,
Is the luckiest dog in the world.

Ashley Reading (8)
Paganel Junior School

THE SUN IN THE SKY

The sun is a ball in the sky.
The sun is yellow which glows in the big, blue sky
That glows in the summer and glooms in the winter.
That shines on me and you.
So shine, shine and shine on me and on you and
Everything you do.

Charlotte Busby (10)
Paganel Junior School

EASTER

Easter is a lot of fun,
Chocolate eggs for everyone,
Girls and boys go out to play,
Searching for eggs on this special day,
They laugh and sing as they play this game,
They're all really glad that the Easter bunny came.

Lyndsay Smylie (9)
Paganel Junior School

STARTING OUT EACH DAY

Mom calls me from my lovely sleep.
I get onto my wobbly feet.
Go downstairs and get a hug from Mom,
Then into the kitchen to fill my tum.
Into the bathroom to brush my teeth then on with my shoes
to protect my feet.
Out the door to meet my friends then into school to learn some maths.

Beth Rose (8)
Paganel Junior School

THE EASTER BUNNY

Hop, hop the Easter bunny's coming
To bring our chocolate eggs
To fill our little tummies yum
Yum, yum, yum, yum you hear the children cry
He's brought a chocolate Easter egg
For every good girl and boy.

Melissa Smylie (9)
Paganel Junior School

GOMA 2002

The long hibernating volcano, like an evil monster from Hell,
Suddenly wakes up with an ear-splitting *roar!*
The flaring flows of lava seek their first prey like a prowling lioness
Stalking her new meal,
The choking gases turn the city of Goma into a vast gas chamber,
The boiling hot geysers shoot out from the ground unexpectedly
Scalding anything that dares to get in its way,
The rock showers bombard awestruck people below like pebbles
Thrown at a huge sea of ants running for their lives,
The continuous clouds of ash block out the sun as if the end of
The world has arrived,
Finally, after a satisfying meal the monster returns to its nap, waiting,
Just waiting, for its chance to strike . . . again.

Geila Alpion (9)
Paganel Junior School

A SCHOOL DAY

Every day I come to school
To learn, have fun and play
But the best thing about school is
It gets better every day.

I meet my friends, send Christmas cards
And treat the teachers good,
It really is a lovely place,
And I behave the way I should.

Athena Sanders (11)
Paganel Junior School

SPRINGTIME

The sun is shining
The sky is blue;
Springtime is coming,
The bees are humming,
Birds are flying,
The frost is dying,
The flowers are growing,
The lawn needs mowing,
People are happy, the spring is here,
They welcome it with cheer,
It seems so long since it was here,
Spring is such a good time of year.

Kerry Martin (8)
Paganel Junior School

THE SUN IS A . . .

The sun is a screw screwed into
the cloud.
It is a badge put into
the cloud.

The sun is a clown's nose stuck
to the clouds.

It is a golden eye spinning to
look around.

It is a meteor falling from the sky.

Andrew Spurrier (9)
Paganel Junior School

THE SUN

The sun is an orange ball
Rolling down the hill.
It is a yellow bulb
Brightening up the sky.

The sun is a bouncy ball
Bouncing round the house.
It is a yellow sun
That shines bright.

Zoe Davies (8)
Paganel Junior School

I WANT A CAT

I want a cat with lots of hair.
I want a cat that shows love and care.
I want a cat that loves me so.
I want a cat that is as white as snow.
I want a cat.

Brogan France (8)
St Dunstan's RC School, Kings Heath

BEST FRIENDS

I walk down the street and I see my best friend
We're going to stay best friends there's going to be no end
We laugh, we play, we have fun all day
We're going to stay best friends
We're going to stay best friends
There's going to be *no* end.

Ailish Erin Prosser (8)
St Dunstan's RC School, Kings Heath

ON MY BIRTHDAY

On my birthday
On my birthday
I get up of course
I have one favourite present.
All my family will be very pleasant.
The best thing about it,
Have no doubt
Your family can't moan or *shout!*
I love my birthday it's really great.
Hip hooray I get to play.
I won't be bored *today!*
It's my birthday
On my birthday.

Leah Costello (8)
St Dunstan's RC School, Kings Heath

SCHOOL!

When you're eight,
When you're eight,
You're always late for school
When the teacher tells you off
You always seem to cough
When you sit down
You've got a frown
Then you get a pencil
When you're eight,
When you're eight.

Connor Kelly (8)
St Dunstan's RC School, Kings Heath

A Young Writer's Dream

It's a young writer's dream
To have all the fame
To beat each other
Or to win the game

It is a young writer's dream
To keep all the bate for me
And to fish out the biggest fish
There will ever be

It is not just poems
As all that I write
It is all imaginable
For it is all needed
Imagination to write
As when I go to sleep at night
I'm just getting ready for the new ideas
I shall be catchin' that very next day

It is a young writer's dream
To win this competition
And to work up a team
And to give all my readers
The gift of a smile
And so I shall gleam.

Michelle Simone Clark (9)
St Dunstan's RC School, Kings Heath

My Mother Said This

'Your eyes are bigger than your belly
Your eyes are bigger than your belly,'
My mother always said
When I'm watching telly.

'I want doesn't get
I want doesn't get,'
My mum is always telling me
When I scream 'Have you got it yet?'

Jessica Stait (9)
St Dunstan's RC School, Kings Heath

I CAUGHT A FISH

I caught a fish
I caught a fish
From my fishing rod
I caught a gigantic one
It had a big fin
It had an enormous nose
It had huge eyes
I caught a fish
I caught a fish.

Alex Carmichael (8)
St Dunstan's RC School, Kings Heath

YOUR EYES ARE BIGGER THAN YOUR BELLY

Your eyes are bigger than your belly,
Your eyes are bigger than your belly,
When you see some ice cream,
You go straight for it,
You will have to pay for it,
Your eyes are bigger than your belly,
Your eyes are bigger than your belly.

Stephen Martin (8)
St Dunstan's RC School, Kings Heath

THE RIVER FLOWS

The river flows
The waves on the river flow red
The river flows
The child on the bed said my ted
The duck on the pond swam upstream
The river flows.

Louis Jobanputra (8)
St Dunstan's RC School, Kings Heath

ANIMAL POEM

The big, brown bear who's really hairy,
Everybody knows he's really scary,
Now there's the monkey,
Who's really funky,
Then there's the lion,
Whose name is Brian,
Last of all there's the spotty leopard,
Who roared at a shepherd.

Andrew Martin (8)
St Dunstan's RC School, Kings Heath

THE SINGSONG POEM

Where's the terrible noise coming from?
Where's the terrible noise coming from?
A terrible noise was coming from you
Where's the terrible noise coming from?
Where's the terrible noise coming from?
That house as we went past!

Rachel Wallace (9)
St Dunstan's RC School, Kings Heath

THE SEA

I watch from the winter garden,
The sea, swirling, crashing,
Splashing, playing with the broken objects,
The fish that lie between the never stopping waves.

Then . . .
A cloud, dark as night, falls over the sea,
Rain pours down over the sea.
I watch from the winter garden,
The cloud goes, the sea is now calm.
It's as if the cloud has told the sea off,
I gaze in wonder.

Marcella Frances Rose Meehan (9)
St Dunstan's RC School, Kings Heath

ON HOLIDAY, ON HOLIDAY

On holiday, on holiday
It is so much fun
I must go for a run
There were seashells, seashells on the seashore
And on the rocks I found some locks.
On holiday, on holiday there was a fair.
Air was blowing in my face.
I tied my lace and I went with a *wow.*
I saw a show at the fair.

On holiday, on holiday
I saw a sparkling light, light
On holiday, on holiday.

Charlotte Kinzett (8)
St Dunstan's RC School, Kings Heath

MIDNIGHT WONDERS

Midnight wonders,
Midnight wonders,
Have you ever wondered
What it's like in space? Well,
I always thought space
Was a little colourful face,
Earth and Venus are the eye
They look alike,
Saturn is the nose,
All the rest of the planets are the mouth,
And Neptune is the tear
Of the universe.
That's what I think about
Space.

Victoria Edge (8)
St Dunstan's RC School, Kings Heath

SUN

The sun is very hot
It's a ball of fire
When you look at it it's like a dot
It will burn a tyre

It is the sun
When you play a game
It is very much fun
All the same.

Ryan Malanaphy (8)
St Dunstan's RC School, Kings Heath

SOMETHING, SOMEWHERE

It was a misty night
As it crept around
The graveyard, it passed
With trees that bowed.

Its unformed back
Shaped mischievously
As it ran in rage
With eyes full of envy.

Ready to hunt
Its mouth for prey
With its other fox
Friends, just like him.

Rema Blake (11)
St John's CE Primary School, Sparkhill

MIDNIGHT HOUR

Something stirred in the midnight hour,
A trifling eye glared in a bush,
An obscure shadow crept across the path,
In a silent hush.

As it roamed in its spot,
The leaves drooped as if bowing,
The trees shook in the moon's light,
Revealing the creature of the night,
The snarling wolf.

Rhianne Locke (10)
St John's CE Primary School, Sparkhill

CLOWNS!

In the big top I was sitting on my seat
I could smell the popcorn I might even meet,
The ringmaster with his top hat and whip
But I was tired and needed a kip,
So I left the big top and stumbled to my hotel
When I saw a clown trying to earn a bit of money I could tell,

But then he laughed a cackle of doom
So I legged it to my room,
I was drenched in sweat and white with fear
So I went to the kitchen and opened a beer,
A ring at the door so I opened it
But it was terrible I bit my lip.
It was a clown with a collecting tin
So I screamed and hid behind the bin.

Philip Davis (10)
St John's CE Primary School, Sparkhill

SNAKES

I was waiting for a good night in,
I was sitting with a big tin
Of chocolate.

The telly was on, the programme started just.
I was enjoying the pizza's crust.

I was having fun until a slithery, slimy thing
Came I shouted 'Blimey.'

It was my biggest fear,
It was a snake, it was right here.

Henna Panchal (10)
St John's CE Primary School, Sparkhill

THE SEA ARMY

The sea draws its army and then converses with its comrades.
Soon the question comes up; how do we do it?
Stealth or head on? The leader decides and then they strike . . .

The sea circles the land and then strikes.
It creeps stealthily up to the bank pilfering debris it can use.
It suddenly shows itself and bolts forward.
It is then, the bank turns into a minefield.
The sea weaves in and out of forgotten debris
Eventually getting to its destination; the defensive wall.
It doesn't lose speed; it instead picks up speed
As it roars into the wall . . .

It lambastes into the wall with such force
The army fly into the air.
The rest of the army retreat as what hit the wall sinks into the sand.
The army flow back into the sea barracks.
They will be back; but they'll be better.

Matthew Evans (11)
St John's CE Primary School, Sparkhill

MIDNIGHT HOUR

All is quiet in the midnight hour,
The night goes blue while the leaves crunch
The creature's eyes shine while looking for its prey
In the depths of the night it scans for its victim.

All is quiet in the midnight hour.
It lurks under the bushes and follows its prey
It lures its victim into a trap.
The moon shines on the cat as it swallows its prey.

Adam Wheatley (10)
St John's CE Primary School, Sparkhill

LEISURE

What is this life if, full of care,
We have no time to stand and stare.

No time to walk up the big hill,
No time to lie down, sleep or chill.

No time to keep fit and play football,
No time to run and play basketball.

No time to play on my Dreamcast,
Like I always used to in the past.

No time to go on holiday,
Whilst I want to have a great day.

No time to go and make Airfix,
No time to play as my dog licks.

A poor life this is, if full of care,
We have no time to stand and stare.

Nathan Numan (11)
St John's CE Primary School, Sparkhill

SNOWFLAKES

From up above the snowflakes saw the Earth
Was dull and grey.
To give Earth some cheering up they settled down
Their crystal flakes.
They saw the Earth from a distance
It looked white as ever and like a giant snowball.

Hiteshree Kundalia (11)
St John's CE Primary School, Sparkhill

THE MIDNIGHT HOUR

It's perched on the tree,
Staring into the dark night and beyond.

It starts to glide into black air.
Its dark and misty eyes looking down
Searching just searching for something.

The leaves dropping as the trees are screaming
As the branches swing malevolently,
While the grass blows wildly.

As it's gliding it sees something,
The night's hunting has just begun
For the owl.

Shiro Miller (11)
St John's CE Primary School, Sparkhill

PITCH-BLACK

Something stirred in the midnight hour,
An eye glowed as it stirred through the darkness beyond,
A distinctive sound came from the darkness
Rattling away with its glowing eyes.

An eerie rattle came from the bush as it went
The leaves rustled then it came out of the bush
It was a deadly sound of a tombstone
And then the shadow crept out
It was a venomous rattle snake.

Vishal Thanki (11)
St John's CE Primary School, Sparkhill

LEISURE

What is this life, if full of care,
We have no time to stand and stare,

No time to see the ball being smacked,
Or see the panes of glass being cracked,

No time to bake, boil or cook,
Or read Delia Smith's cookery book,

No time to see my brother grow,
Or see a blackbird or maybe a crow,

No time to amble in the park,
Or take my dog and hear him bark,

A poor life this is, if full of care,
We have no time to stand and stare.

David Andrew Weake (10)
St John's CE Primary School, Sparkhill

OLD MAN SEA

Old Man Sea is feeling hungry
He leaps from his chair and moves towards
The unprotected beach

Old Man Sea dashes across the sandy beach
Capturing all stones in sight
To call his own

Old Man Sea is satisfied for now,
So off he goes to recline his chair . . .
Until the next time.

Jamie Mullis (11)
St John's CE Primary School, Sparkhill

MEAN OLD SEA

The greedy, hungry sea
Needs some lovely food to eat but how?
To drive as fast a Michael Schumacher
And eat all the people like a monstrous dog,
Or the easy way - flood the land,
No I'll do it the hard way!

The sea spilt over the people
Crushing smacking and flattening them
Like a wild and monstrous dog.

The lonely sea which had enough friends
But now no friends it got,

How stupid could I be?

Zarha Ali (10)
St John's CE Primary School, Sparkhill

THE SEA

Out in the ocean, the sea hatches a daring plan
for his attack on the beach,
absent-mindedly chewing seaweed
and the side of fishing boats.

He charges up the beach chasing jellyfish and crabs,
taking the seaweed prisoner.

When he has enough prisoners,
he will sweep away and munch on them,
planning his next attack.

Rozie Corbett (10)
St John's CE Primary School, Sparkhill

FOOTBALL CRAZY!

Football, football
You are always in the goal net
Football, football
You go faster than a pet

Football, football
You are always there
Football, football
When people don't care

Football, football
I love you
Football, football
I hope you do too.

Nathan Delfouneso (11)
St John's CE Primary School, Sparkhill

SPRING

I saw a spear of purple blood
Dart tip with golden fire,
No reminiscence of mud.

There amongst all the colour
Stood a dull, green spire
Snowdrops ringing their pure white bells
Amidst the verdant green

Spring has come!

Stefan Michael Wrobel (10)
St John's CE Primary School, Sparkhill

THE MIDNIGHT HOUR

Something stirred in the midnight hour
An evil eye glanced seriously into the blank night.
A grey, ugly shadow appeared in the dull graveyard.
The gravestones were moaning and the trees bowing
Full of fright.

The leaves falling because of the creature,
The haunting noise coming through the grey church door.
The creature scaring the dead.

The hunting of the night ends for its prey
The owl flies back to its children.

Heena Jagatia (11)
St John's CE Primary School, Sparkhill

THE MIDNIGHT HOUR

All is quiet in the midnight hour . . .
Apart from one creature on the prowl!
It sneaks through the gates,
Its ghostly eyes glare menacingly,
Its shadow creeps across the graves.

As it passes by the trees
The branches and leaves shake and shiver
Its shadow runs across the graves
As if it were waking the dead.
A night's work was about to begin for the fox.

Chloë Lee (11)
St John's CE Primary School, Sparkhill

SILENCE PREVAILS

Something stirs in the midnight hour,
Silence is not prohibited here,
Although it is very silent.
The creature summons silence as it perambulates
Around the graveyard, stealthily.

As it casts its eerie shadow upon the trees,
The foliage withers.
The tombstones whine as it brushes past them

An ear-splitting scream breaks into the silence
As the fox slaughters its first victim.

Robert Ashley (11)
St John's CE Primary School, Sparkhill

SOMETHING STIRRED IN THE MIDNIGHT HOUR

Something was very windy
I saw something
I jumped. I carried on walking to the shop
Some kind of animal was watching me
I was still then I ran out of breath
I ran out of the rainforest
I stopped and I was very sad
Because it must be a big thing.
I stopped to see what it was.
All it was was a dog.

Lydia Smith (10)
St John's CE Primary School, Sparkhill

THE MIDNIGHT HOUR

Something stirs in the midnight hour,
It creeps, it crawls,
Something creeps in the midnight hour,
It menacingly crawls through the wood,
Something clambers in the midnight hour,
The trees bow down in its glory,
Something crawls in the midnight hour,
The tombstones raise at its sight,
Something creeps in the midnight hour,
The plants view its eerie shadow,
Something clambers in the midnight hour,
The owls view their king, Mr Fox.

Kina Sinclair (10)
St John's CE Primary School, Sparkhill

FEAR

I was looking forward to go to the pet shop.
It was near the top of the road.
The time had come before I was sitting on my bum.
It was light not night,
I was talking while I was walking.
I opened the pet shop door as I said
'What a poor dog.'
There it was a slithering shivering
'Snake'.
I ran out of the pet shop.
'Dad I don't want a pet' I suggested.

Jerome Greaves (10)
St John's CE Primary School, Sparkhill

MIDNIGHT

Lurking in the midnight hour.
As a blurry shadow crosses the haunting graveyard
Eyes glaring at its prey.
Face staying stiff.

The midnight madness forces over the dark.
The tombstones moan and groan.
The leaves crashing into each other, but make no sound.
Trees bowing down like a ghost was about to appear.

Sprinting across, 'yum'.
What a healthy snack for the wolf.

Naomi Bishop (11)
St John's CE Primary School, Sparkhill

THE MIDNIGHT HOUR

There was something creeping in the midnight hour,
It was crawling under the dead, black bush,
The smell of death filled the air.

Its eyes glared around the bushes,
Searching for its prey,
It had brushed past the trees as the leaves shuddered,
Still searching for its victim.

As it drew nearer to its victim,
Everything had frozen,
As they all watched this creature creep upon its victim,
The fox had finally found what it had wanted.

Anika Parmar (11)
St John's CE Primary School, Sparkhill

NO TIME

What is this life if, full of care,
We have no time to stand and stare.

No time to play on my Dreamcast,
Or have a daydream like the past.

No time to see my brother tall,
Nor time to see him kick a football.

No time to relax on my bed
Or give a cuddle to my ted.

No time to stroll in the park,
Or draw a picture of an ark.

No time for the park to play on the swing
Or hear the oven say ping, ping.

A poor life this is, full of care,
We have no time to stand and stare.

Haifa Choudhury (11)
St John's CE Primary School, Sparkhill

WHEN THE WORKBOOK MARRIED THESAURUS

When the Workbook married Thesaurus,
Their wedding had a good chorus,
But the marriage was forced
So they got divorced,
And the Workbook bought an old walrus.

Joseph Greenfield (11)
Stanville Primary School

ISABEL MET . . .

Isabel met a giant cobra
Isabel got an ice cream soda.

The cobra had massive jaws
The cobra's teeth were as big as my cat paws.

The cobra said 'I spit venom.'
Isabel said 'You silly lemon.'

'I kill with one shot
Maybe I'll suffocate you with a pot.'

Isabel Isabel didn't worry
Isabel did not scream or scurry.

The cobra moved side to side
Isabel bit him with all her pride.

Nathan Lowe (10)
Stanville Primary School

THE SUNLIGHT

The sun was shining very bright.
The flowers were opening in the light.
The sea was waving very high
And the sand was blowing in the sky.
I saw a shell which was very bright.
I picked it up in the sunlight.
The grass was growing long and green.
The houses were sparkling clean.

Chantelle Evans (10)
Stanville Primary School

THE ANTARCTIC ANIMALS

In the Antarctic the water is cold, the ice is like frost
And the sea view is bold.
The walruses dance on the icebergs at night,
While the others watch in the moonlight bright.

In the Antarctic the water is cold, the ice is like frost
And the sea view is bold.
The penguins dive into the cold, blue sea,
And a fright I gave them when they saw me.

In the Antarctic the water is cold, the ice is like frost
And the sea view is bold.
The polar bear's fur is white as snow,
I love the way it can glisten and glow.

Abigail Barter (9)
Stanville Primary School

MATT THE CAT

I know a cat
Whose name was Matt
Who sat on another cat.

He was wearing a hat,
Which made him look fat,
Who sat on a bat instead of the mat.
He chased a rat,
Although he was fat.

Michelle Ball (9)
Stanville Primary School

THE SEAGULL AND THE EAGLE

There was a seagull,
Who flew with an eagle,
Over the deep blue sea.
He saw some bees,
Who lived in the trees.
Then the seagull told the eagle
And the eagle said, 'That's illegal
For bees to be living in trees.'
The seagull said, 'I don't think it is,'
The eagle said, 'Well let's have a quiz.'
Some time later in the middle of the quiz,
From the Tweenies, up popped Fiz.
'Now dear Fiz what are you doing here?'
'I just popped up to say hello,
Now I'm going back down below.'
The quiz ended once and for all,
So they both decided to go to the ball.
They came from the ball and went to the mall,
Came from the mall and went home
And they lived in a millennium dome.

Mica Pencheon & Shabana (9)
Stanville Primary School

DOG POEM

I've got a dog as thin as a rail
He's got fleas all over his tail
Every time his tail goes flop
The fleas on the bottom all hop to the top.

Sean Berwick (11)
Stanville Primary School

LOVE

If you were strawberries
I'd be the root to let you grow.

If you were a thirsty flower
I'd be a cloud to rain on you.

If you were a pane of glass
I'd be the picture that you were close to.

If you were a bee
I'd be the stripes that make you look beautiful.

Reece Willett (10)
Stanville Primary School

THE MAGIC BOX

I will put in my box
A special shell called Debris,
A twisted, crooked unicorn's horn
That casts a spell on you,
A dog that flies away and barks.

I will put in my box
A shiny, glimmering, radiant, sparkling crystal shell,
Three violet wishes spoken in Hindi,
A golden, bright mask,
A shiny, glimmering train that sparkles like a crystal.

My box is blue, like the blue of the shining sea.
When I open my magic box,
Everything comes alive!

Adam Teeling (11)
Uffculme Special School

THE MAGIC BOX

I will put in my box
A silver, shiny magic box,
A golden medal with ribbon
And a winning ticket for the lottery.

I will put in my box
A golden mask
With Victorian things in it,
An ancient doll from Mars.

My box is made of
Glittery cardboard with golden scales in it.
The corners are made of cats' claws.

Luke Satchwell (11)
Uffculme Special School

SOLDIER IN THE GRASS

The soldier is lying in the grass,
The soggy grass.
His clothes are wet,
The enemy are coming on their horses,
Black and white along green fields.
The soldier can feel the damp earth.
The soldier fires at the enemy.
A bird flaps its wings, frightened.
The soldier does not want to carry on,
He wants to go home.

Steven Taylor (11)
Uffculme Special School

SOLDIER IN THE TRENCH

I am lying in the long, saturated grass.
My clothes are drenched.
I feel nothing but the spongy, damp, winter soil.

I see the brown and black forest.
I see the sun rising.
I see all the murderers of the evil battle.
I see all the guilty horses
Leading them into battle.

I hear pattering rain.
I hear the horrible shooting of guns.
I want to be innocent and stay at home.

Adam Sutcliffe (10)
Uffculme Special School

SOLDIER IN THE GRASS

I am lying in the long, soggy grass.
I am in a battlefield.
My clothes are dripping wet.
I see my enemy getting closer and closer,
My knees are shaking, I am frightened.
I am getting nervous about killing,
I want to live, I want to live.
I want to go home,
But I have to kill if I want to live in peace,
So I am going to shoot my enemy
When he walks by.

Leon Ming (10)
Uffculme Special School

THE MAGIC BOX

I will put in my box a magic wand
That can make people disappear
And a million pounds made out
Of gold that glows in the dark,
A diamond that shines every time you look at it.
I will put in a snack that helps you with homework
And a lottery ticket for my mom and dad.

I will put in my box
A super ball that can fly all the time
And a crystal ball at the top of my hat.
I will put in gold treasure that
Can transform people into ants
And a magic that makes people come alive.

My box is made of glass and metal
With stars on it.
On my box is a big unicorn's horn that is sharp.
I will put my grandad's photo in it.

David Walsh (11)
Uffculme Special School

MY MAGIC BOX

I will put in my box
A ring that could make snacks
And lunch that gives you money when you eat it.
A unicorn's horn with magic
That could make life easy and you know too much,
A crystal that can do you good.

My box is made of
Shiny stuff and it is unbreakable.
It is cool and heavy,
With a dragon's head for the lid.

David Eling (11)
Uffculme Special School

HOMEWORK

Homework is awful,
It should be made unlawful.
Maths makes me flap,
I feel like I'm in a trap.
English is boring,
You'll find me snoring.
Science makes me weep,
Then you'll find me asleep.
RE is a pain,
It should be run over by a train.
PE makes me sweat,
And it also makes me fret!
They make me go swimming,
But I know I'm not winning.
IT is just great,
A subject I don't hate.
Then there's history,
That's just a mystery.
Geography should never have been invented,
The person must've been demented.
Then there's DT and art,
They make me smart!

Amar Kundhi (9)
Wheelers Lane Junior School

AUTUMN WEATHER

Autumn weather, never mind.
Tipping it down,
Like a watering can.
Weather is bad luck,
Like breaking a mirror.
Autumn weather, never mind.

Autumn weather, never mind,
Falling down
Like a feather falling to the ground.
Weather wicked,
Like snow brooding,
Autumn weather, never mind.

Autumn weather, never mind,
Something blazing down
Like a torch,
Like a beach ball
That you have lost,
Autumn weather, never mind.

Autumn weather, never mind,
Frost has gone,
Like a layer has gone,
There is no mist,
Like cold to an insect,
Autumn weather, never mind.

Lewis Williams (10)
Wheelers Lane Junior School

PENGUIN

A penguin's my name,
I walk like a plane.
I slip on the ice,
That's not very nice.

My claws are like nails,
They can hurt you like hail!
Come over and see
How cruel I can be.

Luke Whitehouse (10)
Wheelers Lane Junior School

TEACHER, TEACHER

Teacher, teacher, sorry I'm late,
I had to clean my breakfast plate.

Then I had to feed the cat,
The dog, the goldfish and all that.

And though I knew I must be quick,
The dog rolled over and then was sick.

After cleaning all that mess,
What happened next you'll never guess.

My baby sister's bottle spilt
And left my homework soaked in milk.

And when my sis' began to cry,
I really couldn't say goodbye.

Things couldn't go wrong anymore,
This was something I knew for sure.

I've run to school, all in a hurry,
But Teacher, teacher, please don't worry . . .

Tomorrow I'll be here at half-past eight,
Teacher, teacher, sorry I'm late!

Tom Reilly (9)
Wheelers Lane Junior School

PLANET EARTH

Look upon this Earth of ours,
So beautiful she seems to me,
But look again with your third eye,
What have we done to this world?
Scarred her with roads and tunnels,
Listen and hear her pain.
The rain is her tears,
The thunder her screams,
Earthquakes her shudder as we build harder.
Why have we done this to this world of ours?
If she were a dog and we were her fleas,
She wouldn't stop shaking and scratching
Till everyone leaves.

Stefanie Brown (9)
Wheelers Lane Junior School

PEACE IS WHAT WE NEED!

Peace is what I dream of,
Peace is what we need,
Not killing, murders or
Such a thing as greed.

In my perfect world there would be angels,
Floating around the town,
To catch disobedient people
Down on the polluted ground.
Nobody would be found guilty of charges,
And everything would be safe and sound.

Aimeé Schörnig-Moore (10)
Wheelers Lane Junior School

IDEAL WORLD

My ideal world would have no stealing, none at all,
A world where shrubs survived and trees stood tall,
A world where birds flew briskly as insects crawl.
That would be my ideal world.

My ideal world would have no injuries and no fights,
A world where men and women, rich and poor, have equal rights,
A world with no factories, or industrial sights.
That would be my ideal world.

My ideal world would have no illegal drugs, not a trace,
A world with enough food for every species and race,
A world where birds flew from place to place.
That would be my ideal world.

Kieran Child (11)
Wheelers Lane Junior School

THE CREATION OF THE WORLD

The world was created and all was peace
And now the world is polluted.

The world was peaceful,
But now it's not
Because the Earth's
Had earthquakes.

People are committing suicide,
What a waste of a life.
And that is my rap of the world.

Jack Reed (10)
Wheelers Lane Junior School

ELEPHANT

I am an elephant,
My desire is to be like you,
To be slim and wear clothes
And eat your food too.

With immense, outstretched feet as big as your head,
My skin of chiselled granite-grey,
Oh what I would give
To go out and play.

I trample everything in my path,
My trunk is distorted and long.
I grunt and groan and honk and moan
When I hear your merry song.

Lucy Blyth (11)
Wheelers Lane Junior School

EUROPEAN RED FOX

I am a fox,
Sleek and sly,
Speedy and swift,
Much faster than the naked eye.

My eyes are like wet marbles,
Put into deep sockets.
I have ears that can hear
The keys in your pockets.

I have fur as soft as snow,
As red as fire,
From head to toe.

Natasha Durrani (11)
Wheelers Lane Junior School

RHINO

I am the rhino, racing around,
Running into a tree and bouncing down.
Up I get, again racing around,
Here I am, a big clown.

I kill prey
And eat his flesh,
With my horn
As sharp as a thorn.

After a day's hunting
I lay down,
The next day,
I do the same.

Rock rhino, the sun sets behind me,
Like a campfire on the horizon.
I sleep like a moon,
Round and rough, bold and black.

Chris Evans (10)
Wheelers Lane Junior School

A POLKA-DOT BIKINI

Sarah wondered
If her itsy-bitsy, teeny-weenie
Yellow polka-dot bikini
Looked a bit funny on
Her massive, dotty, spotty,
Grey and lumpy,
Lardy botty.

Lisa Reilly (9)
Wheelers Lane Junior School

SQUIRREL

He flies without wings,
He jumps without springs,
High in the treetops
He chatters and sings.

Racing,
      Chasing,
           Squirrel.

He tiptoes on branches,
He takes lots of chances,
His tail helps him balance,
Wherever he dances.

Jumping,
      Bumping,
           Squirrel.

He shakes the nuts down,
When they're shiny and brown.
He nibbles them, dropping
Their shells on the ground.

Cracking,
      Smashing,
           Squirrel.

Raghav Jogia (9)
Wheelers Lane Junior School

IF ONLY

If only the sky was blue each day
And clouds were white, no longer grey.
If only disease would quickly die
And people were honest and did not lie.

If only food did not go scarce
And water was always clean.
If only this world was perfect,
But it isn't, how mean!

Caitlin Anderson (11)
Wheelers Lane Junior School

CREATION

C   reation started with light,
R   ight. Next, God created the sky.
E   xcellent, he thought, then made plants,
A   lso land and sea.
T   he sun, moon and stars were next.
I   n the next day, sea and sky creatures came.
O   n the sixth day, mankind and animals came.
N   ow for a rest, thought God, for he had used all his might.

Eloise Foley (10)
Wheelers Lane Junior School

WINTER

When it is winter, you start shivering.
When it is winter, your heart turns to ice.
When it is winter, it feels like you are in a freezer.
When it is winter, you can hear the whispering.
When it is winter, the trees go side to side.
When it is winter, all the leaves fall down from the trees.
When it is winter, the sun falls down.
When it is winter, it gets dark quickly.

Lucy Burns (8)
Wheelers Lane Junior School

TIGERS

Tigers prowl, tigers growl,
Tigers pad, are they sad?
Maybe we'll have to ask
When we come face to face
With a tiger!

Tigers pounce and I bet
They could trounce an
Elephant in a race.
Maybe we'll have to
Check that out when we
Come face to face
With a tiger!

Tigers fish, tigers wish,
Oh I wonder what
They wish for?
We'll have to ask
When we come face to face
With a tiger!

Scarlett Sprigg (8)
Wheelers Lane Junior School

KOALA BEAR

Up there, in the tree!
That creature spying down on me.
His eyes are a pair of searching radar,
Looking for prey near or far.

The koala it is, my pet named Simons,
Look out! Here he comes,
Claws as sharp as diamonds,
Up in the tree he is slung.

He's zooming down the tree
And although eyes as innocent as a child,
A very bad temper has he,
He is never, ever mild.

Daniel Howell (10)
Wheelers Lane Junior School

TIGER

Slowly, quietly
As a small snail,
Then *pounce!*
The tiger strikes dominantly
On an unfortunate gazelle.

Black as night stripes,
Against yellow and orange
Sunset skies,
Glaring, laser-ray eyes,

Staring at you
Like two beams of light.
Now feasting and feast he will,
Happy, joyful, until
He runs out.

Any food? I've eaten it all,
I'll starve to death!
But what's that?
Another gazelle? Yes!
I can feast again!

Joshua Wilson (11)
Wheelers Lane Junior School

HIDDEN TREASURE

Sail the seven seas to the magical place
Where dragons become fairies,
Where goblins become angels,
Where you dig for a box full of treasure and gold.
If you open it up, it's full of all your dreams,
What you wish for most of all.
You'll become a saint there, even the bad,
There's a 99% chance you'll find gold,
So tell all your friends about this paradise.

Carla Hancox (11)
Wheelers Lane Junior School

BROTHERS HAIKU

I have a brother,
He is very annoying
As all brothers are.

Anjali Unarkat (10)
Wheelers Lane Junior School

TIDAL WAVES

Tidal waves come from the sea,
They scare you and me.

Sending ships across the bay,
Sinking ships through the day.

Destroying land is the sea's demand,
Wrecking the Earth for all its worth.

Yousaf Kharal (10)
Wheelers Lane Junior School

MY CAT

My cat is a purr-ball,
Even though she looks like a furball,
Even though she's a little thin,
She's still got really furry skin.

My cat's silky,
Her mouth's milky,
She smells of tuna,
Or would do sooner,
If you'd let her.

My cat rolls on her tummy
To tell us the treats are yummy.
She jumps her paws up
And hooks her claws up
On Mummy's best carpet.

Isn't she a naughty pet!
When I'm sitting down
She jumps up with a frown,
Then after with a grin,
She strokes me with her furry chin.

When we go to bed at night,
She snuggles in her bed, tight.
If she needs to pay a call,
Her litter tray's against the wall.

She wakes up when the day is dawning,
Ready to greet us every morning,
Then she gives her tail a swish
And says, 'Miaow! Please fill my dish!'
Isn't she a naughty pet,
My furry, purry cat!

Robert Williams (8)
Wheelers Lane Junior School

SHARK

Lurking in the dark,
That is the shark,
The T-rex of the sea,
All the fish you wouldn't want to be.

His teeth are butcher's knives,
It's magnificent how he dives.
He's a Ferrari,
A super sight to see.

His tail a powerful whip,
His prey gone in no time,
Living the life of crime,
Submerging down into the darkness!

Nicholas Parry (11)
Wheelers Lane Junior School

BIRD

A bird am I,
Hot and dry,
The blazing weather
Will burn my feathers.

I fly around, hunger is my mood,
There is no menu to choose my food.
There's no dish
Off which to eat my fish.

A bird am I,
I swim in the sky.
A home, a nest,
The only place to take my rest.

Yasmin Moseley (10)
Wheelers Lane Junior School

TIGER, TIGER

Tiger, tiger, burning bright,
Circling the jungle in the night,
What immortal hand or eye
Can frame the frightening symmetry.

Deep beneath the tiger's homes
Is rotted flesh and zebra's bones.
Every animal and every bird
Knows the tiger who can be heard.

When tiger tracks through the grass,
Then no animal dares to pass.
The stealthy tiger who has no number,
Puts any animal in a forever slumber.

Jennifer Barnes (11)
Wheelers Lane Junior School

EARLY MORNING RUSH HOUR

Alarm goes off, oh no, I'm late.
These early mornings I really hate.
Just got time for breakfast, if I'm quick,
Early nights, Mum says, do the trick.

Have a wash, go to the loo,
Rushing around, things to do.
Grab my coat, hat and bag,
These early mornings are such a drag.

Out of the door and off to class,
Hurry Mum, step on the gas.
I hope I'm not late for school,
Oh no, I am! I've broken the rule!

Jade Brooks (9)
Wheelers Lane Junior School

THE SIX SIGNS OF AUTUMN

The first sign of autumn
Is the leaves changing colour,
Gold and bronze leaves swaying in the trees,
Bare branches go up and down
Like a yo-yo bobbing around.

The second sign of autumn
Is the start of hibernation,
Animals sleeping safe and snug,
Outside it's cold and frosty
Like a frosty freezer or fridge.

The third sign of autumn
Is the weather,
The coldness of the whispering wind,
Frost on the window
Like a man's breath.

The fourth sign of autumn
Is the warm homes,
The warm burrows,
The nests are empty as the birds have gone,
Like a stream running away.

The fifth sign of autumn
Is the warmth
Of the fire and cosy cats purring,
As happy as can be,
Like a hot summer's day.

The sixth sign of autumn
Is the start of winter,
No more sun,
No more animals,
Like a deserted town.

Charlotte Huddlestone (11)
Wheelers Lane Junior School

WEATHER

The sky clouds up,
Like a dark, gloomy fog hugging the sun,
Covering up the blue sky,
No aeroplanes could possibly fly.

Now the wind is blowing fiercely,
Like a tornado destroying everything,
Blowing side to side,
All the animals have to hide.

All the rain falls,
Like a waterfall gushing down,
Making puddles everywhere,
Falling through the cold, cold air.

Now here's the snow,
Like white cotton wool stumbling and swaying down.
It's gone frosty and white
Over the freezing, cold night.

Mary Wass (10)
Wheelers Lane Junior School

IF GOD

If we were given power by God,
Then why do we abuse it?
If we were given love by God,
Then why did we lose it?

If we were given resources by God,
Then why do we use them for bad?
If we were given life by God,
Then why do some people act like they never had?

Holly Bruce-Abrahall (10)
Wheelers Lane Junior School

EDDY

I know a teddy called Eddy.
He's cuddly, brown and smelly,
He goes to the pub and drinks lots of beer,
That's my teddy called Eddy.

I know a teddy called Eddy,
He's cuddly, brown and smelly.
He snores in bed so I can't get to sleep,
That's my teddy called Eddy.

I know a teddy called Eddy,
He's cuddly, brown and smelly.
He plays tricks on my dad and blames it on me,
That's my naughty teddy called Eddy.

Would you like a teddy called Eddy?

Rosie Long (8)
Wheelers Lane Junior School

DOGS

Dogs are fun,
Dogs are great,
Dogs are every boy and girl's mate.
They play when they're happy,
They eat when they're sad,
Some even bark, really bad.
But when you have problems,
No friends to talk to,
There's that little dog
Who's there for you!

Kaylea Behan (10)
Wheelers Lane Junior School

POLAR BEAR

I wish I was like you,
But I'm only me,
There's only a few
That I can see.

With fur thicker than ice
And my nose is like a metal protector,
But I can't see any mice,
If only I had a detector.

There I see
A fish over there,
That's for me
I just declare.

I dig in the ice
With my claws of steel,
But it was just rice.
I wish I had a meal.

Amritpal Singh (10)
Wheelers Lane Junior School

MY FAMILY

Boot a-bulging, roof-rack rocking,
Dad is driving, Katy's coughing,
Mum has a migraine, Granny's grumpy,
Sarah swears and sticks up sweeties,
Dan the dog is wanting wee-wees.
All around are cars and cases,
Cones, congestion, furious faces,
Hauling homeward, slowly, slowly,
From a fortnight hardly holy!

Shyam Unarkat (8)
Wheelers Lane Junior School

ANIMALS!

The cat got old,
The dog went blind,
The toad went bold,
The mouse was kind.

The giraffe was crazy,
The elephant saw a dog,
The monkeys were lazy,
The dog sat on a log.

The pig was pink,
The kangaroo was blue,
The toad was playing 'The Weakest Link,'
I wouldn't like that, would you?

The zoo keeper was mad,
The donkey was cold,
The hamster wasn't cold, I'm glad,
The polar bear was bold.

The kitten was talking,
The cow was working,
The cubs were drinking,
The lioness was sleeping.

The monkeys were laughing at a clown,
The snake was clean as a window,
The alligator was shiny as a crown,
The rhino was making a lovely shadow.

Sonia Parveen (9)
Wheelers Lane Junior School

SCHOOL

S chool is what we love,
C heating is what we hate,
H omework is what we all adore,
O ur knowledge is a heavy weight,
O verall, we don't think it is much of a bore,
L ies are what we are to tell.

Maria Tahir (9)
Wheelers Lane Junior School

DOGS

Dogs like to run
And play in the park
And when they get excited,
They begin to bark!

A dog is a man's very best mate,
Especially when they get to
Lick his plate!

Tom Elvins (9)
Wheelers Lane Junior School

SCHOOL

S chool is the best,
C ome to Woodgate,
H ow I love Woodgate,
O h don't be afraid,
O h come to school,
L ook around you, you will love Woodgate School.

Bethan Hawker (9)
Woodgate Primary School

THE INGREDIENTS

The ingredients are
Two eyeballs,
Frogs' legs,
Bogies,
Unicorn horn,
Dog poo,
Cats' teeth,
Rabbit liver,
Goat's brain,
Cow's heart,
Trolls' hair,
Human toenails,
It makes a nice recipe!

Daniel Whitworth (10)
Woodgate Primary School

FIREWORKS

F   lames spurt off as the rocket fires up,
I   love to watch them bang with a hot cocoa cup,
R   ight up in the sky they shatter and explode,
E   ach and every time the timing of the bang seems like a code,
W   hooshing, bang, it hurts my ears,
O   oooh, up in the sky it's smoky when it clears,
R   ight after the fireworks they put on a little show,
K   eeping us entertained although,
S   eeing the fireworks bang all night,
     sometimes they might give me a little fright.

Sam Blount (10)
Woodgate Primary School

FIRE AND CHILL

A crackle, a demon,
The element of Hell!
Burn, crackle, crackle, burn.
A secret identity,
A warm, cosy friend,
Burn, crackle, crackle, burn.

The icy glaciers,
A princess of snow,
Chill, tremble, tremble, chill.
A white cloak
Breaking the barometer;
A sheet of winter,
Chill, tremble, tremble, chill.

Katie Maxted (11)
Woodgate Primary School

SCHOOL

As she walks into the school ground,
Her heart starts to pound.
She knew she had a test in school
And felt like diving into a great, big pool.
She walked into the long, long hall,
Up to her classroom, which was by a wall.
She sat at her desk
And peered at the test.
She went to the playground and
Had a rest from her test.

Rachel Poole (10)
Woodgate Primary School

KEVIN THE COUCH POTATO

Kevin sits there night and day,
You'll be lucky to hear him say,
'Mom, I'm going for a jog,
In the early mist and fog.'

He sits there scoffing his face,
Sitting in that very same place.
Chocolate, crisps, whatever you please,
His belly even goes down to his knees.

Chocolate is his favourite food,
He is a really big, fat dude.
Whenever he has money to spare,
He likes to buy a chocolate pear.

McDonald's is his favourite place,
So that he can fill his face.
He also likes Burger King,
When he gets a chocolate ring.

When he does exercise,
He puts it back on with apple pies.
So if you want to stay alive,
Don't be like Kevin Hive.

Eric Stone (11)
Woodgate Primary School

ANIMALS

Dogs bark when someone rings the bell,
Cats, dogs and rabbits are so fluffy.
Cats go miaow, miaow when someone strokes them.
Snakes are very slimy.

Casey Street (8)
Woodgate Primary School

DOLPHINS

Dolphins are big,
Dolphins are grey,
Dolphins are cool
They swim all day.
I would like one for a pet,
Especially when they're wet.

Lorna Ormsby (9)
Woodgate Primary School

THE STORM

There was a storm and it was so warm,
We had a warning that the storm would be at dawn.
There was a baby who just was born,
But then she got shocked and popped the corn.
People were tired so they had a yawn,
But when they woke up, they saw them torn.

Jonathan Gardner (8)
Woodgate Primary School

TWO LITTLE KITTENS

Two little kittens sitting on a mat,
One was thin and one was fat.
They had their favourite bear,
Then they went to the fair.
They sat next to the merry-go-round
And watched it spin round and round
And round and round . . . until they got sick!

Ross Edwards (9)
Woodgate Primary School

ALL ABOUT KIA

Our baby Kia,
Is rather sweet and dear.
She's learning to walk
And beginning to talk.
We love her to bits,
She has us in fits,
She will wibble and wobble,
Then begin to topple.
She'll fall to the floor
And heads for the door.
She'll climb the stairs
As much as she dares.
She's a mischief maker,
Especially when you wake her.
We love her very much,
Her every kiss and touch.

Jade Anderson (10)
Woodgate Primary School

WINTER

Winter is cold,
Icy and freezing,
Jack Frost comes out,
Makes you shiver.
The sun goes in.
A cloak of whiteness
Covers the houses,
A season to forget.
We await the spring.

Amy Summerfield (10)
Woodgate Primary School

THAT GOAL

Up he picks the ball on the wing,
Sprints like a cheetah,
Powers through the defence like a bull.
One man, two men, three men, four,
The control he has is inspirational,
Sublime,
Beautiful,
The ball glued to his feet.
Here he comes, the toothless keeper,
The striker swerving in and out.
Round the keeper,
Shoots,
Goal!
What gifted two feet he has,
An historical goal,
And they lift the cup for the
First time in twenty years.
The club and I are joined,
This club is my life.

Nathan Morris (11)
Woodgate Primary School

MY FAVOURITE FOOD

My favourite food is
Spaghetti Bolognese,
Stringy and slimy.
Boil the spaghetti,
Boil the stew.
What does it taste like?
Does it taste like me and you?

Adele Winters (10)
Woodgate Primary School

DISGUSTING FOOD

Peas and chocolate pudding,
Custard, sausage and pie,
Salad and fishes eyes,
With some chilli sauce at the side.
Cheese with rabbits' ears,
Cucumber with some beer,
Tomatoes you can pick,
Don't give them to me,
'Cause I'm going to be sick!

Natasha Cordero (11)
Woodgate Primary School

TOAST

Toast with butter, Marmite and jam,
Toast burnt and brown,
Toast with thick, burnt ham,
Toast with pâté, tuna flavour.
Toast, I love it.

Callum Smith (10)
Woodgate Primary School

MY FAVOURITE FOOD

Spaghetti Bolognese, all stringy and white,
Wriggling like worms
With a lumpy, brown sauce.
Twist the worms around the fork,
Into my mouth, it tastes delicious,
Sucking it up like a caterpillar,
Feeling it wriggling about in my tummy.

Tracy Albutt (11)
Woodgate Primary School

FEELING SCARED

I'm walking down the street,
Looking around, wondering,
What's happening in the world?
Then I thought,
Why am I so scared of the world?
I know why,
There's so many bad things happening.
Why can't it all stop?

Kayleigh Smith (10)
Woodgate Primary School

TIGERS

Tigers, they run like lightning
That shines at night.
They hunt for food,
They find a lamb,
Eat it!
Poor lamb.

Kelly Gordon (11)
Woodgate Primary School

CITIES

Day and night in the city,
People rushing here and there,
Working, shopping, looking around,
Crazy people bobbing up and down.
Never silent, always loud,
The city that never sleeps.

Abigail Trueman (10)
Woodgate Primary School

THE BEACH

Beautiful white sand,
Tropical palm trees,
Hot sun blazing,
Cool, wispy ocean.
The wind blows gently in my hair,
The sand is like golden jewels.
I can see dolphins jumping
Through the cool ocean,
The beach is incredible,
It's a wonderful sight.

Samantha Close (10)
Woodgate Primary School

I'VE CAUGHT A COD

Put a maggot on the rod,
Throw it out and catch a cod.
Bring it in with a reel,
Cook it for your evening meal.
Out again you throw the line,
Ready to catch something really fine.
This is the way to escape the wife
And I'm having an easy life.

Adam Williams (10)
Woodgate Primary School

THE GIFT

Born on Christmas Day,
Tiny eyes,
Button nose,
Cries like a whining puppy,
Wanting more food.

She makes us laugh
With her funny faces.
We'll love her forever,
My tiny baby sister!

Bethany Dawson (11)
Woodgate Primary School

THE GOBLIN'S CELLAR

In the goblin's cellar,
It is very tiny.
It's very confined and restricted.
It smells like sick.
There is someone down there,
Is it a boy or a goblin?
What is it?

Michelle Kemp (11)
Woodgate Primary School

SATURDAY NIGHT

It's Saturday night
Down at the ground,
Kicking feet
And a screaming sound.
Thousands are watching,
Awaiting the goals,
They score!
What a roar.
I feel disappointment,
My confidence in my team melts.

Jack Hindley (11)
Woodgate Primary School

THE FLOBBERS

The Flobbers are huge, oversized worms,
That eat small, microscopic germs.
They're friendly really, but they don't look right,
If you encounter one, it'll give you a fright.

They have a beautiful queen (beautiful in Flobbers' terms)
But anyone who meets her will definitely squirm.
She's pompous and rude, never heard of 'please'
She really does think that she's the bees' knees.

One day a poor servant was a little late
In serving soil on a china plate.
In his haste, he walked into a door
And the expensive plate was no more.

'It's ruined!' cried the queen in shock,
As the servant recovered from his knock.
'That was very rare and came from Norway,
This is no good, you'll have to pay!'

'But I am poor!' exclaimed the servant on his knees,
'Please let me off, please, oh please!'
But she turned her nose up at him and said, 'You've got the sack,
Get out of the palace and don't come back.'

'The queen has more money than she needs,
To make me pay, well, that's just greed!'
This is what the servant moaned to his Nan,
She replied, 'I have a plan.'

His nan got the job serving dinner to the queen
And carefully, so she would not be seen,
Put a little drop of oil
On a jug from home which looked fit for a royal.

She served the dinner, feeling quite smug,
And as the queen dropped the jug,
She put on her best acting voice and with false dismay
Shouted, 'That was pure diamond! You'll have to pay!'

The queen looked horrified, but didn't think twice,
She gave them some money (£120,000 to be precise).
The queen had learned her lesson and didn't delay
In giving all her money away!

But really, you would have to be a fool
To not notice the jug wasn't made from jewels.
That jug didn't really have any class,
It was just made from shiny glass.

The citizens rejoiced as the taxes went down.
The news spread around the town,
The streets were once again full of Flobbers and laughter
And everyone lived happily ever after.

Bernice Cameron (11)
Woodgate Primary School

SCIENCE

Science is a perfect subject.
You experiment with different objects.
Science is number one,
Some people think it's a con.
You have to be really clever,
To stay a scientist forever.

Thomas Bathurst (10)
Woodgate Primary School

MY GOLDEN BOOT

Running around the football field,
Got to win that lovely shield.
I was wearing my golden boot,
The ball came to me and I had to shoot.
There it goes, high in the sky,
It came back down and hit the goalie in the eye.
He screamed out in pain
As the ball bounced out again.
With a swing and an aim,
I hit it again,
The ball struck the net
And we won the game.

James Williams (10)
Woodgate Primary School

THE HONDA FIREBLADE

I hear a rumble,
Faster, faster,
It's as quick as a cheetah,
Growling like a monster,
Right over on the bend,
Scraping knee-pads,
I'm the king of the world.
I pull a wheelie,
Opening the throttle,
I go faster,
I feel great!

Laura Bates (10)
Woodgate Primary School

THE GHOST WHO WOULD NEVER GO

In the night,
At exactly midnight,
A very strange thing patted me on my head
And stood at the side of my bed.
I shouted, *'Ghost!'*
It flew down the stairs
And was trying to hide
And tried to touch me with green goo
And my face turned blue.
It was the next day,
In May,
That the ghost
Visited my house,
I was making a cake and was rolling the dough,
When something shouted, *'Boo!'*
My heart went up
And then went down,
He told me not to bawl,
Or call.
I tried to run,
But he grabbed me round the neck.
When he eventually went
At 12pm,
He had made a terrible mess,
For then he went to spook
Mrs Luke
And I never saw him again.

Hayley Smith (11)
Woodgate Primary School

THE SEA

In the sea there are sharks,
There are killer seals as well.
Some nice ones as well.

The sea is bright and blue,
The sea is calm and dangerous.
The sea is very deep.

The sea is full of danger.

Josh Hirons (8)
Woodgate Primary School

MY CAT

My cat
Killed a rat.
We let him out
And he runs about.
My cat killed a bird and had a feast.
He is like a wild beast!

Jake Solomon (10)
Woodgate Primary School

MY PET VACUUM CLEANER

He sucks in like an elephant,
He slides down the hill like a person.
If you press a button, he goes to sleep.
He eats the dirt off the floor.
Every day I feed him some dirt.

Sabeel Mahmood (9)
Yorkmead J&I School

MY PET OVEN

My oven is like a pet.
It cooks and makes me food.
It makes all things nice.
It sometimes eats my cake.
It has got six eyes,
Everyone turns its eyes upside down,
It's got no shoes.

Henna Bhatti (8)
Yorkmead J&I School

MY PET RADIO

My radio is like a pet.
She talks to me when I am lonely,
She has got two big blue eyes,
She eats tapes and CDs like a flat doughnut,
She has got a silver nose.

Shelley Kempson (9)
Yorkmead J&I School

MY PET RADIO

My pet is like a radio.
She drinks oil,
She eats tapes.
When she's happy, she sings.
When she's angry, she won't work.
She stands around,
We stroke her every day.

Ravina Parmar (9)
Yorkmead J&I School

MY PET CAR

My car is like a pet,
She has lights for eyes,
She winks at her friends.

She runs around when she's happy
And talks like a human being.

When I'm sad, she says,
'Do you want to play cards?'
This makes me happy.
She's a funny car and
Only two people can fit.

When I'm stuck on my work,
She helps me with it.

Sandeep Kaur (8)
Yorkmead J&I School

MY PET AEROPLANE

My aeroplane is like a pet,
It drinks fuel,
It has a tail,
Long wings,
But no feathers.
When it's sad, it glides,
When it's happy, it flies.
When it doesn't drink, it dies.

Kassim Din Ayub (8)
Yorkmead J&I School

MY PET AEROPLANE

My pet aeroplane,
He has wings on each side like a bird.
My aeroplane has a pointy nose which is very sharp,
He has a fish's tail which stays still.
He lives in the blue sky.
He has eyes which are black, full of glass.
I love playing with my aeroplane.
He plays with me when I am sad.
He eats lots of fuel to make himself healthy,
He glides through the air.
My best toy is my aeroplane.

Nandani Khunti (8)
Yorkmead J&I School

MY PET AEROPLANE

My aeroplane is like a pet.
He has long falcon wings,
A sharp shark's tail,
A pointed nose,
Two glass eyes
And he drinks oil.
He takes me wherever I want,
He sometimes makes me rich.
He lives in a garage near my house.
His name is Tommy
And he can fit twenty-three people in him.

Aaran Chauhan (8)
Yorkmead J&I School

MY PET OVEN

My pet oven is like a pet.
He lives in the kitchen.
He eats potatoes, broccoli,
And if he doesn't like them,
He burns them.
When he pants smoke,
The reason is he's warm.

Pradeep Singh (9)
Yorkmead J&I School

MY PET RADIO

He lives on the shelf in the kitchen.
He drinks out of a cable with hot, dangerous liquid.
He tells me the weather and time,
He keeps me company.
He falls asleep sometimes, then he wakes up and sings.
He doesn't like getting wet.
His favourite food is very flat pizzas with holes in.
I love my pet very much.

Alex Marsh (9)
Yorkmead J&I School

MY PET RADIO?

He eats rectangles with snakes on top of them,
His big head opens to replace his brain,
His aerial goes up and goes down,
His three arms go in a hole,
He goes to sleep and wakes up,
My pet has two cages on the sides.

Prabhjeet Singh Wilkhu (8)
Yorkmead J&I School

MY PET BICYCLE

He has wheels like two ears,
He has handles like two hands,
He has a seat for his face,
He has a reflector for his nose,
He eats dust and he is a bicycle.

Usmaan Ali (9)
Yorkmead J&I School

MY PET BICYCLE

My bicycle is like a pet,
He rolls on his wheels.
I put my feet on his pedals,
I sit on his seat and I hold his hands.
When his pedals stop going round,
They go tick, tick, tick,
And he has got a ding-a-lingy thingy
Called a bell.

Sultan Lohar (9)
Yorkmead J&I School

MY PET BICYCLE

My pet bicycle has two enormous eyes,
My bicycle tings and lives in an old garage.

He is my friend,
He ticks like a clock when I change gear.

His eyes keep swirling around crazily.
He eats my trousers.

Lisa Dearn (9)
Yorkmead J&I School

IN THE PLAYGROUND

In the playground
You can hear the wind blowing in the trees,
You can hear the crisp packets rustling on the ground,
The doors banging!
The children are wrapped up warm
And running out to play.
The teacher blows the whistle now,
It's half-past ten
And the doors bang again.
There is total silence in the playground,
You can even hear a pin drop.

Neelum Hunjan (10)
Yorkmead J&I School

SOMEWHERE IN OUR SCHOOL TODAY

Somewhere in our school today,
The teacher's going dotty.
There's a new girl in the nursery,
She still wants her potty.

Amy's eating cheese and Jade's fallen on her knees,
Now my teacher's really mad
Because the children in my class
Are really, really mad.

Somewhere in our school today,
The building's really quiet
Because it's that time, but wait,
Now it's ten to nine.

Danielle Kiernan (9)
Yorkswood Primary School

SPRINGTIME

Flowers are pretty,
Violets are blue,
Roses are red,
Beautiful too.

Plants are growing,
I can see leaves,
I'm watering my plants,
I've rolled up my sleeves.

People are joyful
Because of the plants,
One thing that spoils it,
Is the disgusting *ants!*

The sun is shining,
The grass is green,
I think this is
A better scene.

Aiden Eaves (10)
Yorkswood Primary School

SPRING

Spring smells so sweet,
It's as lovely as a bee,
Ladybirds pop out,
Flowers grow around,
Chrysalis pop open
And butterflies pop out.
I love this season,
Without any doubt.

David-John Whitlock (7)
Yorkswood Primary School

WHALE SONG

Whales are a lovely sight to see,
Swimming so gracefully,
But now they are endangered
And we are to blame.

We show no emotion,
Just sending out oil ships into the ocean.
Sending pollution down into the depths of the sea,
Killing and injuring these wonderful creatures.

Many tales have been said
Of people whose hearts are made of lead.
We just think of ourselves,
We just want money and nothing else.

Whales are wonderful, they belong in the sea,
So why kill them, can't you see?
These creatures do not need to be killed,
They need to stay in the ocean!

So when you're out at sea,
Just think how it would be
Without any creatures, including whales,
In the oceans any more!

Rebecca Cartwright (10)
Yorkswood Primary School

MY TWIN COUSINS

My twin cousins are a real pain,
They're only babies, so they don't use their brain.

My twin cousins live with their mum and dad,
If they leave, they will be very sad.

My twin cousins are fat and chubby,
Sometimes they get very grubby.

All these rhymes are really true,
And I love my cousins more than you!

Laura Holden (9)
Yorkswood Primary School

MY ANGEL

My nan's an angel,
She watches me.
She's up in Heaven,
But she can still see.

She wears a pearly dress
With diamond wings,
She holds a harp
And sometimes sings.

I know all this
'Cause in my dreams,
She visits me,
Her smile it gleams.

I wish I could meet her,
Face to face,
I guess on Earth
Is not the place.

My nan's an angel
She watches me.
I bet she holds
Heaven's key.

Sherall Jopling (10)
Yorkswood Primary School

THE MONKEY

There was a brown monkey
Who swung on the tree,
He had no friends,
Apart from me.

He wanted to make friends with the snake,
He wanted to make friends with the hare,
He wanted to make friends with everyone,
But nobody was there.

He made friends with the hare,
He made friends with the snake,
He made friends with everyone,
Even the fish in the lake!

There was a brown monkey,
Who swung on the tree.
He had a lot of friends,
Just like me!

James Clark (10)
Yorkswood Primary School

THERE IS SOMETHING IN THE ATTIC

There's something in the attic,
What can it be?
Is it a hamster?
Is it a snake?
Is it an ant?
I don't know,
Now go and see.
Ow, help! It's a monkey!

Jessica Holloway (10)
Yorkswood Primary School

SOMEWHERE IN OUR SCHOOL TODAY

Somewhere in our school today,
The quiet secretary is checking
The black, leather register.

All the tiny Year 1s are having an interesting science lesson,
Whilst the bigger children in Year 5 are having
An intense game of kickball rounders.

Somewhere in our school today, a Set 1 history class
Are watching an amazing Kenyan programme.
During a very boring English lesson, a young, tired boy
Is snoozing whilst he's getting called by the teacher.
A clever boy named James answered 12x12
In a vital maths lesson.

Somewhere in our school today, a boy is listening carefully
To the annoying rules of an important game.
SATs are coming, SATs are coming, so revise on your books.

Somewhere in our school today, all this happened in class!

Christopher Hughes (10)
Yorkswood Primary School

PERFUME AND FLOWERS

Flowers are pretty and this someone is too,
Perfume smells nice, but my brother loves goo!
The smell of perfume is ever so nice,
This someone very special would scream if they saw mice.
The colour of petals shining so bright,
This someone's pretty face glistens like a sparkling light!
This someone very special, very special to me,
Can you guess who that can be?

Jemma Dickenson (10)
Yorkswood Primary School

MY BEST FRIEND

My best friend is fair and sweet,
She is like a special treat.
We play and play and play
Together each and every day.
She always sleeps at my house,
Always as quiet as a mouse.
My best friend is very kind,
We keep treasures you couldn't find.
We never keep secrets from each other,
We always spy on my smaller brother.
My best friend is very kind,
We keep treasures you couldn't find.

Angela Swann (10)
Yorkswood Primary School

SOMEWHERE IN OUR SCHOOL TODAY

Somewhere in our school today
Mr Male thundered at the ignorant child.
The paint-splattered artists were
Enjoying making a terrible mess,
The frustrated teacher sighed at the puzzled class.
My friend's embarrassed red face lit up the room.
The puzzled pupil bit her lip,
The curious girl was determined to read about volcanoes.
All this happened in our school today.

Kirsty Norton (9)
Yorkswood Primary School

THE SUN

The sun is blazing on my back,
Like a huge fireball,
Scorching his rays
On my small body.

I had my sunglasses on,
Reflecting in the sun,
Sipping lemonade,
Rocking, burning, fun.

Now it's going home time,
In the midnight sky.
I hope it's this weather all the time,
Never the pouring rain.

Nicole Byrne (10)
Yorkswood Primary School

DO THIS, DO THAT!

Mom says, 'Do this,'
It gets on my nerves!
Dad says, 'Do that,'
It gets on my nerves!
My brother says, 'Do this and that,'
It gets on my nerves.
Any more of this and that,
It will get on my nerves!

Jade Coleman (10)
Yorkswood Primary School

UNDER THE SEA

Dolphins dashing through the waves,
Sea horses hiding in the caves,
Oh how nice it would be
To live under the sea.
Starfish are spinning,
Big fish are winning,
Oh how nice it would be
To live under the sea.
Shoals of fish keep moving,
Little fish are soothing,
That's how nice it would be
To live under the sea.

Jessica Bates (10)
Yorkswood Primary School

PLEASE SIR!

'Please Sir,
Can you look at my work?
I hope you like it.'
'Ugh, it's covered in dirt.'
'No Sir, that's a picture.'
'Doesn't look like a picture to me,
Copy it again for the competition that's free.'
'Sir, it'll take me ten minutes.'
'Well boy, you've got to hurry.'
'It will be done, Sir, don't worry!'

Niall Pocock (10)
Yorkswood Primary School

FOOTBALL

Football is the best sport,
I play it every day.
I mostly play up front,
I play all year and in May.

I support Birmingham City,
I really must say.
They always win,
Every day.

Their colour is royal blue,
West Brom fans say Blues are poo!

Lewis Williams (10)
Yorkswood Primary School

THE SHARK

There was a huge shark
Who lived in the sea,
He looked at a fish,
He looked at me.
He snapped at the fish,
He snapped at the sea,
He snapped at a log,
He snapped at me.
He ate the fish,
He drank the sea,
He snapped at the log,
But he didn't eat me!

Matthew Jones (9)
Yorkswood Primary School

AN ALPHABET POEM ON CHRISTMAS

A   is for advent calendar with pictures and chocolates,
B   is for birth of baby Jesus,
C   is for candles that light up the dark night,
D   is for decorations on the Christmas tree,
E   is for elves, they are Santa's little helpers,
F   is for family and friends who join you for dinner,
G   is for gifts that you are given,
H   is for happy faces of little girls and boys,
I   is for icing on top of the Christmas cake,
J   is for jolly faces of moms and dads,
K   is for kindness to your family when you give gifts,
L   is for love which means people care for one another,
M   is for mince pies that are yummy,
N   is for nice chocolates that you eat,
O   is for ogres, they are big monsters,
P   is for presents that you unwrap,
Q   is for quilt, it keeps you warm,
R   is for reindeer which fly high in the sky,
S   is for Santa who gives you a present,
T   is for trimmings that are hung on the ceiling,
U   is for under the mistletoe where everyone kisses,
V   is for Valentine you kiss,
W   is for wardrobes, they are full with new clothes,
X   is for Xmas Day and there is snow,
Y   is for you, dreaming of a white Christmas,
Z   is for zest for the Christmas fun.

Sarah Hall (10)
Yorkswood Primary School